The Pregnant Guy

SIMON MORSE

Parentlink PubLishing
17 Carpenter Street
5th Floor
Singapore 059906

Cover illustration courtesy of Candy Gourlay
www.mumatwork.co.uk
Book design: Jonathan Gullery

ISBN: 978-981-05-8392-7

ACKNOWLEDGMENTS

WELL IT SURE ISN'T hard to know where to start. None of this would ever have been possible had my lovely wife not bullied and brow-beaten me into having a child and making me "The Pregnant Guy" in the first place. So my greatest debt of gratitude has to be to her, not least because she said so. And not just for making me a father — the best job I have ever had — but also for selflessly allowing me to record and then recount all of the ridiculously stupid things we did on our one-year journey from deciding to have a baby, through to actually achieving her, I mean our, goal.

I also have to thank my daughter, just for turning up. She knew, and still knows, nothing about the book that was written to mark her passage into the world. By the time she learns how to read, I can only hope she will also have learned understanding and forgiveness. Reilly, I'm sorry that you ended up with me as your father. You deserve a lot better. I, on the other hand, could not have dared hope for more.

Next in line is my friend and colleague Brendan. As an author who has actually *been* published, he more than anyone was aware of the pitfalls of being stupid enough to try to write a book. But his enthusiasm and encouragement never once wavered, along with imparting a great deal of extremely sound advice that I am quite relieved I followed.

I must also thank my tireless editor Natalia, the first unfortunate soul who had to read this book in its entirety and try to make some sense out of it. I thank her for the numerous idiosyncrasies she had to translate into something intelligible and for the arduous task of correcting all of my wandering tenses. That she had to endure all of this madness while herself being pregnant was the most amazing feat of all.

I should also give special mention to my own family. My father, mother and sister are all unfairly ridiculed by me in this book in the name of artistic license — and frankly I quite enjoyed doing it. My parents naturally have to share a portion of the blame for the way I turned out, so they really can't complain too much. Instead they're putting their efforts into trying to ensure I don't mess up their granddaughter. My sister can take the moral high ground and simply rest on her laurels, knowing that she has proved to be a much more capable parent than I can ever hope to be.

Thanks to all my friends and colleagues, who encouraged me and kept reinforcing that this was a project worth finishing. Many of us were starting to think my daughter would have a child of her own before that day ever dawned.

Lastly, I thank you, the reader, for sharing in my journey. Having chosen this book, I can only presume that you are embarking on a similar adventure of your own, for which I wish you all the luck and happiness that only a child can bring.

Contents

INTRODUCTION

" **P** REGNANCY? I'M A GUY. I don't need to read a book about that," you may say. That was my first mistake, too. "What for? I'm not the one that's pregnant," you argue. Technically true, but in reality you're about to be swept away on the roaring tide that is your wife's pregnancy, as helpless as a one-legged man at an ass-kicking contest.

So why read *my* book?

They say people learn from their mistakes. If that's true, then absolutely no one learned more about pregnancy than I did. Because on the day that little stick turned blue, my knowledge and interest in anything baby-related ranked right up there with Stevie Wonder's contribution to darts.

Yet I survived. And by sharing the multitude of experiences I was subjected to — you will as well.

For I wasn't just the guy who said he probably wouldn't ever have children, I was the guy who *knew* he would *never* have children. Parenthood was going to be the first event in my life that made an unmedicated trip to the dentist the preferred choice.

One of the first things I learned was that although much is known, and has been written, and has been talked about incessantly, on the subject of pregnancy and its effect on *women*, little has been unearthed about what happens to the *male* of the species during this creative evolution.

Like many guys, I presumed that I'd just be able to muddle through the entire process, making it up as I went along. Who would notice?

A casual glance around the house at the crooked paintings, wobbly furniture and the flashing timer on the video recorder should have reminded me of the fallacy of that concept. As my best friend always says, RTFM – Read the Manual.

Any man who finds out that his partner is pregnant is akin to a little kid at Magic Mountain who is about to take his first ride on "The Black Hole." He's fully aware that he is going *on* a roller-coaster, but he has absolutely no idea *where* it is going. Never mind the shock of the sharp curves and the sudden, rapid descents, even the simplest of turns will come out of nowhere and frighten the crap out of him. Sure, many will get off and immediately want to go on another ride, but others will simply throw up.

Although devoid of actual knowledge with regard to being pregnant, I was able to develop a theory very quickly, which went something like this:

It is not just the woman who goes through pregnancy. As if by osmosis, the man is drawn into it as well. We may not be a seahorse (the only one of God's little creatures where the male carries the baby, as far as I know) but we have to live, and most likely endure, vicariously every single little change that a woman undergoes. We men may not experience the symptoms, but we sure get to suffer all the consequences.

Now, I'm not saying that this is in any way unfair (much).

After all, we were there right from the start of proceedings, however briefly, and should see it through to the end.

Mind you, let's not forget that a woman is designed to get pregnant and have a baby. It is entirely natural in the truest sense of the word. Women are maternal long before they ever become pregnant. Some men struggle to become paternal even after the children arrive, in the same way they take years before they start to behave like men, despite adulthood having come upon them.

So, can my book help? Were you lucky to have chosen this? Perhaps it would be more accurate to say this book is extremely lucky to have been chosen.

There is such a multitude of titles out there on the subject of pregnancy, the odds of you picking the best one are really quite staggering — probably somewhere up there with winning the lottery.

Purely on that basis, you might as well end up with this particular version than any other. Yes, I know that you'd rather have won the lottery, but I promise at least that by purchasing this book you have not diminished your chances of becoming a millionaire. And on the bright side, it will give you something to do while you wait for the money.

Of course, if you're buying this book because either you or your partner is already pregnant, then your chances of becoming a millionaire have already been reduced to almost zero by the cost of raising children.

Speaking of long odds, if you're a fellow "Pregnant Guy" reading this book, I'd be prepared to bet there's only about a

1000-to-1 chance you actually bought it yourself.

The number of men buying books about pregnancy is roughly equal to the amount of women who purchase books on testicular cancer. Granted, the women don't have quite such a range to choose from. Although Amazon's selection of 2,595 books on the inner workings, or lack thereof, of the scrotum is an almost unbelievably large number and has got to be a lot more information than the average person wants or needs. I realize Lance Armstrong's amazing recovery has made the whole subject popular, but there's a limit. You would certainly hope none of these books are illustrated.

Not only that, but it would take the bravest of men to weave his way through the protruding bellies in a store's pregnancy section to find such a book, should he ever actually want one. Eyes would burn into the back of his head, saying "watch it buddy, it's your lot that put us here in the first place."

Because of this, the vast majority of books on pregnancy are bought by women. And it seems they use the same criteria for choosing what to buy as a Frat Boy does when getting alcohol for a party: Quantity is a sure-fire winner over quality. Better to have 12 bottles of whisky than a 12-year-old scotch.

Luckily, indiscriminate grabbing of pregnancy books by the armful is made much easier by the fact that another quick search on Amazon.com reveals 38,257 choices on the subject — and that's not counting this one. If you go into your local Barnes and Noble, there's at least one whole aisle dedicated to the topic and evidently, that only carries a fraction of the repertoire available. (It may just be my imagination, but I'm sure the pregnancy aisle is slightly wider than all the others, in deference to the clientele.)

There are countless books on every conceivable — if you'll excuse the expression — facet of pregnancy: How to get pregnant; how not to get pregnant; what to wear, eat, and drink and what not to wear, eat and drink; how to stay fit and not get fat, up to and including a book on what to do when you get fat anyway. It would seem that regardless of whatever a woman knew and experienced in life up to the point when she became pregnant, she will now have to learn everything all over again and will need intensive instruction. Anyone would think pregnancy was a condition that lasted a lifetime rather than a mere nine months. Mind you, there were certainly countless times when I thought that to be true.

If a woman should prove to be a tad indecisive (and suffice to say that indecision is an affliction befalling almost all pregnant women) and were to browse through the entire selection, she would most probably have given birth before she had made her final choice of reading material.

Because of all these reasons, it's no great surprise that a woman tends to buy a multitude of books, much in the same way as people like opting for the random selection with lottery tickets.

This randomness theory does have one attribute working in its favor as far as men are concerned. It would be a worry if we knew our wife had specifically bought a pregnancy book for Dad-to-be. The action would suggest an insistence of male involvement from a very early stage that would undoubtedly only get worse as the pregnancy progressed.

However, by relying on the quantity over quality technique, men can deduce it was by total chance that this particular book ended up in the pile. We may actually get back a few brownie points by looking at it, rather than worry about facing a written exam on its contents at a later date. (I say "back" because we know a man's bank balance as far as brownie points are concerned can only ever be in debit. We can win some back and climb toward zero, but we lose them at such an alarming rate it's impossible to ever get in credit.)

Should a woman actually get as precise as looking at the titles, hopefully she will have a few reasons to choose this book in preference to some others. Just by including the word "pregnant" in the title, I have a book that creates an instant appeal to the female half of the adult literate population. In the same way, any book with the word "Golf" on the cover will prompt some interest with almost all of the other half.

Secondly, she may have a curiosity about what she can expect from her partner as they go through pregnancy together. Or more importantly, what she can order her partner to do for her while she is pregnant. The next, and probably most important reason, is the fervent desire for her partner to learn something about the numerous ordeals a woman has to go through during pregnancy and childbirth. Then he will surely be able to empathize and support her every step of the way and understand why she has gone completely batty.

Of course this is a ludicrously optimistic aspiration right from the start, and most likely a fatally flawed concept.

It's the same principle that makes a woman buy the book "Men Are from Mars, Women Are from Venus" by John Gray. She wants to read it to better understand her man so as to be able to improve their relationship. And by that it usually means she wants to find out a man's weaknesses so that he can be more easily controlled and manipulated into doing what she wants.

Then she also expects her man to read the book in order for him to better comprehend the many intricacies and quirks of his beloved woman, so that he is better equipped to give her what she craves, desires and needs. This would then remove the requirement for him to be controlled and manipulated.

In my view, where women seem to go wrong is that if they read the book carefully to start with, they would realize there's not a snowball's chance in hell that most men are going to.

I hereby offer my sincere and unreserved apologies to Mr. Gray if I have in any way caused offence or misrepresented his book — which has sold a billion or so more copies than this ever will — as I'm sure it's by now quite apparent that I have not read his book either, much to my wife's disappointment.

To prove it is nothing personal against Mr. Gray, I also would like to state for the record that I have not read, nor have I the slightest intention of reading, "Chicken Soup for the Soul" by Jack Canfield, or any soup for any other part of the anatomy, for that matter. Again, I'm sure Mr. Canfield has written an excellent book, or indeed many books, whereas I have done neither, so it's not my place to criticize. All I'm saying is that it's not my cup of soup.

I didn't check through the 2,595 offerings about testicular cancer, but what are the odds there's a "Chicken Soup" for that too? However, I was very pleased to notice there is a "Chicken Soup for the Golfers' Soul," which wins the plaudits from my earlier point about how to generate mass appeal for a book: Chicken soup for the woman, golf for the man and you've got the entire adult world covered. Nice going Jack. Combining "pregnant" and "guy" was the best attempt I could come up with to achieve the same goal.

And yes, since you asked, there is indeed a "Chicken Soup for the Expectant Mother's Soul," although Mr. Canfield may have made a tactical error there by not getting the word "pregnant" into the title. All I can say is, Jack must be a revered man in the soup industry and about as popular as Colonel Sanders among the chicken fraternity.

I very much doubt that this book will be as informative as any of the above mentioned titles.

However, for those men who are about to embark on the adventure of parenting for the first time, I hope that my experiences will demonstrate to you that even the most reluctant and idiotic of participants can not only survive this ordeal, but even prosper. Failing that, you can always fall back on the old adage that nothing cheers you up like the misfortune of others.

One thing I can tell you for certain. By the time my lovely wife gave birth to a brand new little soul, a *very* different guy from the person I had been nine months previously was also born.

Chapter 1

THE DECISION

"WE'RE GOING TO HAVE a baby," my lovely wife said, while studying my face for any hint of a reaction like a skilled interrogator. Now I understood why she had given me the very large glass of South African red wine that I was currently hiding behind. I took a long, slow gulp. From my wife's expression, I could tell she was expecting a response, and she wasn't looking for my opinion of the wine.

You may well be baffled by my hesitation. After all, when one's wife tells you she's pregnant, the reply should be obvious and immediate, with "that's fantastic darling, I'm so happy," being a clear winner over "is it mine?"

But here's the catch: She wasn't pregnant. So, as I already knew for certain that her comment was not a statement of fact, I was only left with the chilling reality that things were much worse than that. It was instead a declaration of intent.

The "baby" discussion was one that had reared its ugly head more than once before. And unfortunately for any baby that would be plucked from my gene pool, "ugly head" would almost definitely be the correct expression. The Oxford University Debating Society could learn a thing or three from the two of us as we entrenched, or as is the fashion since the Iraq war, embedded, ourselves at the opposing ends of the argument.

Naturally it's not hard to deduce that my wife was firmly in the camp that was in favor of the motion, while I was landed with the task of putting up a defense. It could be billed not only as the consummate and eternal battle of the sexes, but also as a conflict between emotion and reason. Again, no prizes for guessing which one of us represented which.

My first salvo was to raise the very valid point that having a baby is an enormous financial commitment, not to say burden, with various studies putting the figure somewhere up near half a million dollars, which I gently reminded my wife we did not have. In fact, we were barely scraping by on what we earned then, I said, and I wasn't blessed with a job that had a great deal of financial upside.

More to the point, for some time I had been nurturing a vision of my retiring at 50, which meant that I was already rounding the final corner and looking down the home stretch. Having had an early start in my working life, after more than 30 years at an office I thought I would need and deserve a break.

If we were to have a child, that would most likely be the end of any retirement plans, early or otherwise, as I would need to work well into my seventies to pay all the bills. (Hence the book idea. Thank you if you bought this copy, shame on you if you borrowed it.)

I had considered this a shrewd tactic with which to start my defense, as it wasn't an out and out rejection of the procreation declaration, but rather just a case of bringing up one of the pitfalls of such a course of action. In boxing parlance, I was keeping my guard up and protecting my chin from potential knockout blows.

My wife continued probing with the jab. Basic, but effective.

"I want a baby."

Perhaps my first barricade had been too self-centered. After all, an early end to my working life would also bring about the premature demise of my pay check, which was hardly something that benefited my wife. It would also mean I would be around the house a lot more — something else I doubt she was overly looking forward to.

So my next attempt was to choose something that also would be a sacrifice to her, rather than just me. I talked about the freedom we currently enjoyed as a childless couple: The ability to go where we wanted, whenever we wanted, with little or no planning or notice required; the wonders of travel and how much we liked to spend time just with each other; her dream of the two of us following the Formula 1 circuit for an entire year. All things we could do together as a couple. And equally, all things that would be consigned to a 20-year moratorium were we to become a threesome. Again, defensive rather than aggressive, and practically neutral in terms of whatever leanings I may have had on the subject. I thought I was playing a very gentle game of Devil's Advocate.

The subtlety was lost on my wife, who stuck with the more straightforward approach.

"I want a baby."

I realized that I was going to have to raise my game a bit as my wife's staccato technique was proving a tough nut to crack. This would mean I was going to have to be somewhat self-deprecating, but that was a price I was fully prepared to pay.

I brought up the subject of age. Not hers of course, as that would have been suicidal, but my own approaching dotage. I was already in my forties, surely a bit long in the tooth to be starting a family? Some of my peers had teenagers by now and were counting down the years to their offspring leaving the nest and flying off to college. For them, the finishing line was finally in sight. A few more years, a big 18th birthday party and throw the kids out on the street to earn their own living — job well done. Did I want to be the next runner in the relay, picking up the baton to start my lap when they had already finished?

I didn't fancy the prospect of turning up at the school gates at the end of the day and having someone ask why my child was being picked up by Granddad. Or the disapproving looks I would get from parents in their late twenties or early thirties who would presume I was some dirty old man that had knocked up a young girl and was now having a second batch of children.

Another straight left was thrown out by my wife, which I thought I was ready for. But I was completely taken unawares by the right cross that swiftly followed. She had upgraded to combination punches and my advance had been knocked back a few steps.

"But I want *us* to have a baby."

It was the use of the "us" word that was the painful blow. All credit to her. It was a cunning tactic to drag me over onto her side of the argument. With the use of one word, it wasn't a fair fight any more. Rather than just her against me, now it had become me against her and us. Suddenly I was outnumbered. If I caused dissent, it was now not merely that I disagreed with her opinion, but my crime had escalated to being divisive to us as a couple. I was coming between "us." It didn't matter that my part of the us had not given approval to be used in this context. The punch had been thrown and I had a bloody nose.

Any thought I may have had of fighting a technical battle and winning the decision, even a split-decision on points, disappeared from my head as the fog cleared. I was behind in the fight, well behind, and there was only one thing for it. I was going to have to suck it in, step it up and go for the knockout, the Hail Mary, the killer punch. Wind it up and let that sucker fly.

"Honey, have you forgotten that I've had a vasectomy?"

Ladies and Gentlemen we have a winner! There it was, a Technical Knock Out in the fourth round, thank you very much. Game over. The fat lady is singing. Elvis has left the building.

No doubt she *had* conveniently forgotten that rather pertinent fact. And I had to confess I was secretly enjoying the irony that my emasculation had come at her insistence. Years ago, after I had convinced her of my total commitment and dedication to never having children, and her apparent acceptance of it, she had suggested I should get the snip, supposedly so that we would never need to have the very same conversation we were now having. I was firing blanks, but she had loaded the gun. Bearing in mind the current situation, I had to concede it was one of her better decisions.

I put on my best poker face, as this was certainly not a time to look smug and victorious. You could even say it was a pyrrhic victory, as I would take no pleasure in seeing my wife crestfallen and upset. I viewed it as the lesser of two evils. I looked at my wife lovingly, ready to console her in her moment of defeat and sadness.

Oddly, she did not look remotely defeated or sad.

"That's no problem these days. There are ways we can deal with that easily enough. If that's your only objection, then I don't see any reason why we can't start working on it straight away, as it may take some time and you're worried about your age as it is. I'll make an appointment at the clinic for you."

So there it was. The game was evidently not over, Elvis was still very much in the building, and the fat lady had apparently barely approached the microphone.

I had sent my 100 mile-an-hour fastball down the pipe, over the corner of the plate and she had hit it out the park for a grand-slam. When your best stuff isn't good enough, what can you do?

I have to confess I still can't actually console myself to either losing the argument or conceding victory, but it appeared that once again my wife had taken advantage of her casting vote in the event of a tie to pull out the win. I also don't recall how she managed to get said privilege in the first place — I suspect she used her vote and the "us" technique to create a two-to-one majority against me.

Anyway, the decision had apparently been made. We were indeed going to propagate the species. This was going to force some changes.

Chapter 2

CHANGES

MY FIRST THOUGHT WAS that I would have to go down to the library to return my favorite book: "How to Retire in 10 Years." I would also have to advise them that this book needed to be re-categorized and placed in the "fiction" section. I would then enquire as to the location of the "frightening reality" department, for the books I would now require. After scanning countless rows of titles, I decided on "Working 'til the Day I Die, or Possibly Longer" and "How to Survive on Two Hours of Sleep a Night — Non-Consecutive."

My dream of a $150,000 open-top sports car would also have to remain exactly that. It almost brought a tear to my eye. That *car* was meant to be my baby. And it had been getting so close, with only another $149,500 to save. Now it looked like the only soft-top vehicle I would be buying was a baby-stroller with a hood attachment. People say you pass your dreams onto your children — I hadn't even fulfilled any of mine yet and already they were being mortgaged for future generations.

My next thought was of our friends. We would have to throw them a big party. A farewell party to be precise, for all of our friends who also didn't have children. Because once you cross the one-way divide into the world of parenthood, those childless friends you once had are left behind in a previous existence and disappear faster than someone who owes you money.

People who have children will let you go on and on about your child because next it will be their turn to tell you how much better their offspring is than yours. People without children haven't got a clue what you're talking about, and while they may sit politely through the first rendition, they won't hang around for the encore.

Fellow parents give a knowing smile as a seemingly normal person buries their nose in a baby's diaper, or peers inside as if there's some mystery as to what they're going to find. The non-parents instantly conjure up pressing reasons for their imminent departure, while deleting your number from their mobile phone.

With this stream of consciousness having taken about 15 seconds, it was time for my mind to return to thinking about sex.

For most men, the revelation that your wife wanted a baby had one saving grace. If you were going to have a baby, you were also going to need to have sex. And not just once, unless you were incredibly unlucky. Friends had told us that doctors say not to be disappointed if a woman doesn't fall pregnant within a year. What man would be? A guy is going to be granted the "Access All Areas" pass, with the added bonus of the potential for demands being made at obscure times with inventive positions, and you think he's going to rush it? That's simply not going to happen. They would be having sex so often it would be quite nostalgic, like before they were married.

I gave myself a mental slap. While delivering my unsuccessful knockout punch during our discussion, I had of course reminded my wife of a rather pertinent piece of information about the fact that down in my baby-making factory, someone had blown the bridge. There would be no Access-All-Areas pass for me. I was going to help make a baby, but I wasn't even going to get any sex out of it. It didn't prove any consolation, but I certainly felt like I'd been screwed.

Probably just as well, my wife would say.

I am the man who is not even entrusted with hanging a picture, fixing anything that doesn't work, or even changing a light bulb. Usually I have been involved in causing an appliance to be in its defunct situation to start with. So as far as my wife was aware, there wasn't the slightest chance in hell that I would have been successful in the ultimate responsibility of getting her even a little bit pregnant.

Just as Captain Kirk would probably never have made it past corporal without the multi-talented Mr. Spock, I too would have to rely on my very own Science Officer to ensure the mission did not end in failure. Otherwise, my character would be the hapless lieutenant from the security detail, who we all know is going to die a horrible death before the first commercial break.

We would be availing ourselves of the wonders of modern technology and having what is called an "assisted pregnancy."

Getting an assist in basketball or hockey is a good thing. Needing an assist for pregnancy does not shroud a guy in quite the same glory.

It transpires there are three basic techniques to choose from, all of which are conveniently referred to in acronym form so you can't remember which is which. Those alternatives were IUI, IVF, and ICSI. (You never know when this may come in handy. You don't want to agree to the wife getting IVF thinking it's a new digital service on cable.)

There is one factor they all seemed to have in common and that was the surgical removal of vast quantities of money from your bank account without the use of anesthetic.

IUI, which stands for Intra Uterine Insemination, is the simplest of the three, even if it does sound more like a disease. As far as I could tell this was the medical equivalent of a leg-up. The man is required to get all warm and cuddly with a plastic cup and provide a sample of his precious life-giving fluid. I say precious in the context of what it can achieve when used correctly. I fully realize that most men in their youth have wasted gallons of the stuff while practicing, frequently solo, for the greater purpose they may once be called upon to provide.

Anyway, the sample is put into what the medical fraternity refers to as a pipette, and what most women would compare to a common turkey baster. The donation is then placed inside the woman's uterus with a fair degree of accuracy, increasing the chances of her becoming pregnant. After all, the less distance the little fellows have to swim to get to the Promised

Land, the more energy they're likely to have left to get the job done when they arrive.

All pretty simple and straightforward, and for the most part, a fairly painless experience all round. The men may have to suffer some minor embarrassment should they come back out of the cubicle rather too quickly with their offering; or pick up a copy of Gardener's World as their reading stimulus of choice; or worst of all get sent back for a second attempt having returned a cup that is still almost empty.

Because of this ease of operation, it is also the cheapest of the three alternatives, which immediately puts it high in the rankings. However, be wary of the wolf in sheep's clothing. Things that appear cheap often have hidden costs. If something seems too good to be true, it usually is. So what's the catch?

It's this. And it's a whopper. While simple and cheap on the wallet, you also have to consider the social cost involved. As described earlier, this is a basic leg-up to help a couple get pregnant. The obvious curiosity among friends and family is which partner is the one that needs the assist.

Taking away the romance, the woman basically had done to her what would have happened during normal intercourse, except with a greater degree of accuracy. But as her "internals" haven't been messed around with, it's a safe assumption that everything is pretty much in working order. So, by a process of elimination, that means it's the guy who has the problem.

Now that in itself may not be an issue. Some guys have deficiencies they couldn't possibly have known about or done anything to avoid. There are cases where men who were given mercury fillings in their teeth later had problems with fertility because of the traces of metal that seeped through their system over the years. Nature moves in mysterious ways and there's certainly no shame in that.

So it's the details of the actual technique used that will reveal the extent of the problem. Here's where the trouble starts. The only real "assistance" given is to place the sperm further along in its journey than would otherwise be the case. This could perhaps be because they simply don't swim very well. Hardly complimentary, but certainly not the end of the world. But how long will it take for people to work out the other possibility? Maybe the reason the sperm had to be put further up the tunnel of love is because his *own* turkey baster was too short to get the job done?

Oh yes. You had better believe it. That's exactly the verdict the women are going to come to, and sooner rather than later. The next time that guy is at a party and he sees his wife talking to a bunch of women who all look at him and smile, his paranoia is going to go into orbit. He will just *know* they are all whispering about how well endowed he *isn't*.

My wife is under permanent orders that whenever women get around to the subject of "size," (and they seem to be prepared to talk about it far more frequently than they're ready to actually take some active involvement with it), she must fervently declare that it does matter, and it matters a lot. If any woman says that it doesn't, we all know what conclusions can be drawn about her husband.

So there's the dilemma. You can save a chunk of change by taking the IUI route to pregnancy, but you'll have to live with the fact that everyone will know you've got a small dick.

Next up the scale is IVF, which stands for In Vitro Fertilization. Now you have to admit this one sounds more like it. It even has the word fertilization in the title, which has to be a good thing, doesn't it?

The main difference here, to use an analogy, is that if IUI is an "In-House Seminar" procedure, then IVF is an "Off-site" event. The necessary ingredients are removed from each of the participants and put to work in a laboratory-controlled environment. The theory is that once these two groups get together, they know what to do and all that's required is to give them some privacy, come back a little later and hopefully find a fertilized egg ready and waiting. This egg is then placed back into the woman and as long as it holds — Voila, she's pregnant.

The advantage here is there's little chance that the sperm is going to get lost or tired along the way as he's airlifted straight to the drop-zone. Secondly, as with IUI, the element of precision with which the egg can be placed back inside provides the optimal chance of success.

Obviously this system requires a greater amount of surgical intervention and has a price-tag that is commensurate with that reality. On the plus side, there's no apportioning of blame to either party, as both are going through a very similar procedure. So with a higher bill comes the benefit of an intact male pride.

ෙ෯

Last on the list, but by no means least, is ICSI, which stands for Intra Cytoplasmic Sperm Injection. As with IVF, it's another off-site event with Mr. Sperm and Mrs. Egg meeting up in the Petri dish. But from here, things start to differ. Nothing is left to chance. Mr. Sperm is not granted any privacy, and is not even left with the option of perhaps being a little shy, or maybe even gay. He gets scooped up and stuck into that egg whether he wanted to or not. If there's a version of male rape, this would have to be close to it.

From the egg's side, if she had some romantic notion of holding out for Mr. Right, or planned on waiting until she was married, she's fresh out of luck. Too bad sister, you're pregnant. Once again, the fertilized egg is then put back where it belongs and everyone waits to see whether it plans to hang around.

We decided to go with ICSI. My view was that it had the most letters of the three options given to us, so by default it must therefore be the most scientific. Was it also the most expensive? Well of course it was.

Take away all the scientific mumbo-jumbo, remove all the bells and whistles, and this little excursion had proven to be basically just another glorified shopping trip, so why should anything be different?

So there you have it. My wife was getting pregnant, and I wasn't even getting laid. The one saving grace was that at least no one would be able to laugh about my penis.

Chapter 3

THE PROCESS

WITH ALL THE INEVITABILITY and appeal of a tax bill, the day had finally arrived. We were off to the clinic to talk with the experts, although I presumed most of the talking would be done by them: A bunch of people who make a very good living by discussing the failings of your genitalia. Pregnancy by committee — it was just going to be a whole load of fun.

Having done our research, we had informed the medical team (which seemed big enough to look after a president rather than a non-descript couple who simply wanted to get pregnant) of our choice to go for ICSI. The assembled group looked at each other with furrowed brows and gave each other earnest nods of agreement. Well of course they did. Unprompted, we had just voluntarily ordered the most expensive offering on the menu. Thankfully, there was no need for them to break into the full-on sales pitch to try to get us to upgrade.

Despite saying that we had indeed done our own fact-finding, we were still to be blessed by the luxury of the doctor explaining to us in excruciating detail exactly what the whole process would involve. This seemed to have been done to achieve two goals. The first was simply for him to show off his boundless knowledge. The second was to give a long-enough explanation to make it appear that this procedure was sufficiently complicated to justify the inordinate amount of money they were going to charge us for the privilege of having our insides toyed with by complete strangers.

Most of what he was droning on about seemed to be almost totally directed at my wife and none of it sounded very pleasant. So I drifted off into a little world of my own for a while, as I knew I wouldn't be living in it for much longer. Five or more minutes must have passed by before a phrase broke through to my consciousness.

I asked the doctor to repeat whatever it was he had just said, because he could not possibly have said what I thought I had heard him say. He duly repeated it for me more slowly, smiling ingratiatingly like I was some little child, too simple to grasp the words he was emitting from his powerful brain. The sentence was indeed almost exactly the same as what I thought I had heard the first time. Much to my dismay, I had not made a mistake.

They were going to inject my wife with *hormones*.

Surely, it was all a cruel joke. I looked around the expensively furnished office, trying to see where they had hidden the candid camera. I know I am not a medical expert by any stretch of the imagination. I wasn't even very successful at "doctors and nurses" when I was a kid, although I blame it all on the nurses. But this just didn't seem to make any sense to me at all.

If you asked me to name one thing that I would have said she had in abundance, it would have to be hormones. My wife had more mood swings than an overworked trapeze artist and blamed all of them on her hormones, as if it was an acceptable excuse that pardoned all sins.

So, in their infinite wisdom, the medical gurus had decided the best course of action available was to shoot her up with a load more, just for fun. It ranked right up there with having free doughnuts at Weight-Watchers, or an open bar at an Alcoholics Anonymous meeting. (And speaking of them, why is it that when you go to a meeting — apparently — the first thing they make you do is stand up and tell everyone in the group your name? What's anonymous about that?)

Sorry, back to the hormones. Were they similar to vitamins in that there was a range through the alphabet that all did different things? A sort of Heinz 57 varieties? Did hormones come in different shapes and sizes? If so, one strain must be particularly virulent, because the same hormones seemed to be invoked every time on behalf of my wife's defense. Did good hormones balance out the bad ones — a sort of battle between good and evil of hormonal proportions?

Not for the first time, I was confused. How could this possibly be a good idea? Even if it was a good thing for my wife, I had a nasty suspicion that it certainly was not going to benefit me.

The medical theory went like this: My wife would be given a series of hormone injections to put her ovaries into full production so they could "harvest" as many eggs as possible. Over the following month, she would apparently produce more eggs than your average battery hen.

I wanted to know why. Were they suggesting that having taken a look at us, it was a long shot that we were capable of making a baby and they needed a legion of reserves to improve the odds? Or perhaps the opposite? Were they thinking that with a couple of fantastic human specimens such as ourselves, once we put our genes together to create a child, it would be so amazing that everybody else would want one just the same and we could start a franchise? Perhaps they were preparing enough supply for the Christmas rush?

I had to remind myself that we were simply trying to have a baby, emphasis on the singular word "A." We were not attempting to breed a football team or start a dynasty. I also didn't think that we would be allowed to create three or four candidates, choose the one we liked the look of the most, and throw the others back. My wife had already stipulated she only wished to have one egg implanted, rather than the two or three that is the normal procedure, as she wanted to rule out the possibility of twins. As every branch of her family tree had twins running through it, this had seemed a sensible precaution to me and one of the few suggestions I had been able to agree to immediately. Actually, it was also one of the few suggestions I had even been asked to give an opinion on, so I was glad to have got it right.

๏๏

The doctors had advised us about the chance of success being more in the realm of possible rather than probable, something in the region of 30 percent, which was why they suggested getting more eggs than was probably necessary. I instantly feared that we would be keeping these guys on retainer and coming back to pay repeat fees as we had attempt after attempt at the baby lottery.

Or even worse. My hysteria was growing to the extent that I suddenly had visions of "The Boys From Brazil" and some evil cloning factory. Were we unwitting accomplices to some mad scientist's devious plot to breed a new super-race? Were we having a baby, or helping a human experiment? How many babies could you have at one time before you had to start referring to them as a litter? Was my wife going to turn into some sort of Queen Bee that had no need for the male of the species once he had impregnated her? Didn't Queen Bees rip out their partner's genitalia after sexual intercourse? Oh well, why should I be scared of that? The way this scientific process was unfolding, she seemed to have precious little need for me to impregnate her in the first place, so that really shouldn't be a worry.

But before I start to complain too much (too late already?) let me admit that things were very definitely shaping up to be worse for my wife than for me. This series of injections was not going to be your average flu jab. Once again, I was somewhat relieved to be the proud owner of a "Y" chromosome.

Daily injections in the lower abdomen for two weeks are

not many people's idea of fun. It sounded more like she was being treated for rabies. I can only presume they had to be given there to get the closest proximity to the target area, similar to the U.S. military laser-guided smart bombs.

I didn't even want to be the one to give them to her, let alone be on the receiving end. This was not because I was squeamish in any way, but simply because I did not want my face associated with causing my wife pain. Sooner or later, I would have to run the risk of the subsequent retaliation.

At least the injections certainly seemed to do the trick. By the end of the two-week program, she had developed a decent-sized beer gut. What an unexpected bonus. This process actually was bringing us closer together as a couple — physically at least.

After yet another visit to the doctor — we now had a season ticket — he determined that the human incubator that was once my wife had laid enough eggs for our requirements. Finally, it was time for the "harvest" and hopefully the Thanksgiving. Not surprisingly, my wife's celebrations didn't extend to cooking a turkey and inviting the family over for dinner.

But the good news that she had finished her two weeks of painful injections was still tinged with sadness. Now it was my turn.

When a man reaches climax, research tells us he mobilizes more sperm-soldiers than the Chinese army for a mission that needs to be completed by one solitary trooper to ensure success. It was not hard to deduce from this fascinating piece of information that these boys are probably not the most intelligent life-forms the world has ever produced.

When you consider how hard it is for some couples to achieve pregnancy, you realize that despite quite astoundingly favorable odds, the usual result of this army of warriors is total and abject failure. Add in the fact that nature, being aware of the male's deficiencies in the area of direction-sense, had helped them out, and it's all the more amazing. To be on the safe side, either of the routes a sperm can take on its journey to Egg-Ville lead to the correct destination, making it quite remarkable that the vast majority of them never turn up at the intended location.

Much as we men would like to think of our soldiers as being Green Berets, or perhaps more appropriately Navy Seals, it seemed they bear more resemblance to Iraqi conscripts. While we envision them forging their way upstream with all the speed, power and finesse of world-record holder Ian Thorpe, they're more likely to be floundering in the shallows like Eric "the Eel" Moussambani from Equatorial Guinea, who only learned to swim the year of the Sydney Olympics in which he competed. (He didn't win.)

Using the analogy that "In the land of the blind, the one-eyed man is king," it was reasonable to assume some among this multitude must be less dense than others. These were the ones who had noticed that every time an army was sent off to war, none returned. They had learned that when the "Attention on Deck; Battle Stations" siren wailed, it paid to loiter at the back of the pack and let the young, eager soldiers volunteer for the front ranks.

They had heard the rumors that countless numbers of their comrades fell victim to the "latex of mass destruction," a weapon the pope himself was still trying to get banned. While others perished on missions that were doomed from the start because of bad military intelligence: "Go back! It's a trap. These are tonsils!"

The bad news for me was that these high-powered sperm were the elite soldiers we needed to maximize our chances of success. And if they were not going to come out for us voluntarily, then we were going to have to go in and get them.

Naturally, this was a far cry from the way the doctor described what was going to happen. He had used a whole bunch of Latin words that I didn't understand, but trust me, this was basically what they were going to do.

My initial relief that at least it would be my wife going through painful surgical procedures, while all I had to do was offer love and support, had disappeared in a puff of smoke.

They were going to slice open my scrotum.

Now I'm sure that there is not one single man that needs to be told that this was the opposite of good. You didn't need a great mind or possess a very developed imagination to work out that this was going to hurt — a lot. Unfortunately for me, I needed no imagination at all. Being a fully paid-up, tie-wearing member of the Vasectomy Club, I had already experienced the dubious honor of having had my scrotum ripped open once before. Both I and my scrotum were fully aware of the fate that awaited us, and we were both shrinking just at the thought of it. The wheels were up and the undercarriage had been retracted.

What the doctor actually said was that he needed to "aspirate some sperm." It seemed to be such a fine, gentle word, aspirate. It sounded like a happy little fellow, very friendly. To aspirate some sperm conjured up visions of setting them free. I was sure that if I was a sperm, I would want to be aspirated too.

The dictionary defined the word to mean "pronounced with an exhalation of breath." No problem there at all. Breathe away. Its neighbor, "aspiration" was even better: A strong desire to achieve an end, an ambition. Lovely stuff, positively uplifting. On with the aspiration I say.

Hang on a second. There was another definition down at the bottom here, almost an after-thought, hidden away at the foot of the page where they had hoped no one would notice it. "To draw fluid by suction from a vessel or cavity." Now that didn't sound so good at all. I didn't like the word suction, at least in this context. I also had a nasty idea I knew exactly what vessel or cavity they were talking about.

The doctor assured me it was a simple operation and would only require about a one-inch incision. "*Only* one inch?" Who was he trying to kid? What happened to all this modern technology and micro-surgery stuff? Where were the optic cameras and the key-holes? ONE INCH? They sure as hell didn't carve that big an opening the last time. Could it really be this much trouble to get my soldiers out? What was he going to use, a spoon? I was not a happy man and quite worried I wouldn't be a man at all after this operation.

By now I had taken an intense dislike to my doctor. My wife's gynecologist had a much more pleasant air about him. Could we get him back please? What kind of man chooses to specialize in a profession where you cut people's scrotum open for a living anyway? It was just not normal. And I thought dentists were bad enough.

He was still talking. I heard something about "a delicate surgical procedure." Yeah, right. Nothing about it sounded delicate to me. My scrotum was delicate in the extreme, and he was planning to re-enact the Texas Chain-Saw Massacre on the poor little thing. And I had to pay for this torture?

Whenever the whole childbirth subject comes up, the girls never miss an opportunity to remind us guys that it is the most painful experience in the history of evolution. Mere men probably couldn't even tolerate it without a general anesthetic, while women can manage it in the back of a taxi if need be. All of that may well be true, and the guys are certainly relieved we got to pick first when God was divvying out the chores. But let us remember one thing. Women were at least designed with the intention of bearing children. I was *not* designed to have my soldiers violently ripped out through a gaping hole the size of the Grand Canyon cut into my scrotum. If I was, it would have a zip.

Naturally, I said nothing of the sort. It wasn't as if I was going to get any sympathy from my wife, who had spent the past two weeks being a pin cushion. My scrotum was on death row, and the state my wife was in, it wasn't even going to get a last request granted.

೦೦

If there was one benefit of taking the scientific route to pregnancy, and I was beginning to wonder if there was, it was that you too get the chance to play the mad professor and join in the proceedings of creation. I was not merely invited, but positively encouraged to attend the ceremony of my wife's egg removal. Metaphorically speaking, I was being asked if I wanted to drive the combine harvester.

As if auditioning for an episode of General Hospital, I was dressed in a set of doctor's overalls, shower cap and face mask. Blue is apparently my color, so instantly I thought I looked more intelligent and no doubt handsome.

Upon entering the operating theatre, I could see my wife was already lying in wait, legs akimbo and strapped into a pair of stirrups that John Wayne would never be seen dead in. She looked more like she was in training for a space shuttle launch.

The gynecologist was sitting where the horse would have been with a tray full of shiny kitchen utensils. I was directed to the talking end, except thankfully she wasn't because she was already under sedation (now if only you could do that at home). In between the doc and me was the monitor for the optic fiber camera. I would be able to see whatever he was doing as well as he could.

Oh yes. I did not fail to notice the discrepancy. Flashy,

modern, state-of-the-art optic-fiber technology for my wife. Blunt spoon for me. And if you think about it, she basically has an open door. Out of the two of us, who was the one that needed all the benefits of modern technology, I ask you?

The camera monitor showed a honeycomb-shaped object. Each segment apparently was a little sack of fluid with an egg inside. It was like an Easter hunt for grown-ups. As the doctor put in the needle, it appeared simultaneously on the screen and inched its way forward. It looked quite blunt as it slowly forced its way through the outer layer of the sack and into the middle. It reminded me of the magicians who stick a needle through a balloon without bursting it. The doc then pulled a wire on the handle and the world's smallest vacuum-cleaner sucked out all the fluid, which presumably also contained one of our most valuable eggs. Forget Fabergé, these were precious.

It only now occurred to me how much it really would have helped if I had listened when they were explaining all of this. I watched intently as one after the other, the little honey-comb sections shriveled and disappeared as they were sucked dry. First the right ovary was drained, then the left, like a bee collecting pollen from flower to flower.

While all this was still going on, the retrieved fluid was taken into the next-door lab where another technician got to work separating the eggs from the liquid. On a separate monitor I could see her trying to grasp hold of each egg with what looked like a miniature grappling hook. It reminded me of when I was a kid, chasing the last pea across the plate with my fork. She shouted out her progress, sounding like the short-order chef in a busy diner.

"I've got one egg," she cried. "OK, three eggs now from the right side. Four eggs!" All that was missing was the ping of the bell to tell the waitress that the order was ready.

I'll have mine over-easy with toast on the side, I wanted to reply. For once, discretion won the day and I kept silent. Even though my wife was unconscious, she would have heard me if I'd said something that stupid.

We finished up with six eggs that the lab technician deemed to be in the best condition and therefore most likely to get successfully impregnated.

All six would be fertilized. We would use one straight away, and the others would be frozen and kept on ice until needed. Even if my wife became pregnant with the first egg, the other five would be held in storage until after the baby was born, just in case anything went wrong. It was a horrible thought. I chose instead to imagine five little Austin Powers in their cryogenic state, waiting to be thawed out so they could save the world from Dr. Evil, the name I had now given to the guy who was going to tear apart my scrotum. Ouch, baby, ouch.

The experts seemed happy enough with themselves. We had half-a-dozen eggs and we were ready to make some babies. My wife, still sedated, was wheeled off to the recovery room. I went to follow her, but was politely restrained by the doctor. The eggs were only half of the equation. They were going to need some soldiers. My time had come.

I can't tell you very much about what happened next, as I

too was put under anesthetic, and lots of it. While I slumbered, they peeled open my ball-bag with the medical equivalent of a can-opener and dug out a spoonful of hopefully what was the best selection of sperm I had to offer — The Rhodes Scholars and the Heissman Trophy winners. My boys would then be taken to the lab, where they would be washed and polished and made to look their finest, before being put into a line-up to see which six super-sperm would be chosen to go on a great adventure and fulfill their destiny.

As soon as I woke up I checked to make sure everything was still present and correct. I was relieved to discover there was no zip.

๏๏

The fertilization process was like a blind date in a Petri dish. "Sperm, meet egg. OK, no hanging about. Get on with it. In you go and do what you do. Go make an embryo, or you will be in the sink and one of your friends will be having a go. There's an awful lot of you guys and only six eggs, so take your best shot."

These poor little sperm didn't even get a chance to practice their foreplay. First, their tales were cut off so that they couldn't escape, probably by my doctor, who liked inflicting torture. Then they were pushed into an egg, whether they liked the look of it or not. This may have been science, but there was no time for chemistry.

As if the sink threat wasn't bad enough, these poor soldiers didn't even get told they still had an 83 percent chance of ending up in an ice cube. However, whether through responding to pressure or a simple eagerness to please, we duly ended up with six fertilized eggs. Six tiny little embryos, ready to go back to the nest.

All of this was done while I was still in a happy dream-state, in a world where I didn't have a big hole in my scrotum.

Or let me sum it up another way. Not only did I fail to be allowed to have sex with my wife in order to get her pregnant, technically speaking, I wasn't even conscious when it happened!

๑๑

As part of the extra service you get for having chosen the ICSI technique, the eggs are kept in the laboratory until the fertilization process can be confirmed. Nothing is left to chance. Once that had happened and we had a batch of fertilized eggs, the strongest candidate is selected, avoiding a possible one-way trip to the deep freeze. The lucky egg then needs to be put back from whence it came in the hope it will snuggle up and get comfy for nine months while it grows into a little person.

So a few days later, once again we returned to the doctor's clinic and my poor wife was put back in her space shuttle position awaiting take-off. I was again invited to watch, although this time I found it much more comfortable to stand. This last procedure was at least the simplest, as the medical turkey baster was used to squirt the egg onto an ideal spot in the uterus.

We had now reached the single most critical period of the entire campaign. So I was more than a little worried to discover it was also the time when the wonders of modern science and technology, for which we had paid a King's ransom, seemed to disappear into thin air. Both the gynecologist and the lab expert reassured us as to the impending success of their endeavors with nothing more than a hearty "fingers crossed."

That was it? We were up to the 21st century; we had put people on the moon; we had cloned a sheep, and the best they could come up with was a paltry "fingers crossed?" I wanted a rebate. They could at least have said "legs crossed."

But it was not to be. That was our lot. With the aforementioned fingers still symbolically crossed, they pushed us politely out of the door and sent us home. With everything we had been through, it ended up being down to Mother Nature after all. Worse than that, we were faced with a two-week wait to discover our fate.

For anyone who thinks the nine months of pregnancy is a long time, I can assure you it was nothing compared with the agony of those two weeks.

It struck me as all very ironic that couples like us, who had to go to seemingly great lengths, and very painful lengths, to get themselves pregnant, were subjected to a further two weeks of suffering before they found out their destiny. For the majority of people, the only delay was the time between realizing you probably were pregnant and popping down to the drugstore and back with a test. For these lucky people, the tension was but a few moments, and they would tell you even that short time was traumatic enough.

It was also perverse that the chance of someone actually being pregnant seemed to be inversely proportional to how much they wanted to have a baby.

The one-night stand; the indiscretion at the office Christmas party after too many cocktails; the broken condom; the optimistic "I've run out of the pill, but it'll be ok." These are all the scenarios we just know have an almost racing certainty of ending up in pregnancy. I'm not including couples who are on the rhythm method, because they are just asking for it. Especially most Caucasians, because if they had ever seen themselves out on a dance floor at a nightclub, they would know they didn't have any rhythm.

The pregnancy test is the only one in life these people took and actually wanted to fail. There is no joy in getting a pass, even though it comes with a prize. That is why the most often repeated phrase before some guy asks the question "Will you marry me?" is "Honey, I'm pregnant."

Here's another irony. While a man's involvement at the initial stage is vital, once we have done our bit, we quickly become a very peripheral figure in the story. There is really not much a man can do for the next nine months, apart from being a constant outlet for his wife's rage. Sure, our broad shoulders are needed to bear the burden of being permanently in the wrong for the best part of a year, but most of us have had some practice at that. So we try to take it all with good grace and a smile. We would be happy to do more.

That's why it seemed to me it was so unfair that the woman

gets to take the pregnancy test. Now obviously, I could see the logic of why it *is* the woman who takes the test — I didn't skip all the biology classes in school. But come on, let's just think about it for a minute. Peeing on a stick. If ever there was a job that was tailor made for the guys, then this would have to be it. I absolutely knew I could do this way better than my wife: Put it further away; hold it up high; move it around. I'll still be able to hit it and with ammo to spare. I can even write my name in the snow, a feat that in the battle of the sexes is very rarely equaled, and certainly not by girls with names as long as Veronica or Henrietta.

My point was quickly proved by the yelp from the bathroom, followed by the sound of plastic on porcelain and a faint splashing noise. My darling wife's aim had been about an inch off, so she had hit her hand, causing her to drop the stick into the bowl, hence saturating it and rendering it useless. Strike One.

Being the cautious type, she had bought two pregnancy tests, so we were immediately ready for another try. Tangentially, why did she only buy two? The need for more than one had become instantly apparent, but any guy would have bought at least three. What would we do if the results had been one "yes" and one "no" and we had no way of playing a decider?

Anyway, with the first one having gone down the toilet, literally, everything rested on the second attempt. It was a pressure shot. Ask Tiger Woods what it was like sinking an eight-footer on the 18th green at Augusta. There were no gimmes.

A positive result is shown by a darker line appearing in the window of the now peed-upon stick. Now you would expect this line would stand out like a nun at a brothel. As we watched, the faintest, weakest little line you have ever seen started to appear. In the history of lines, this thing would not even get a footnote. It was like playing "Where's Waldo?"

Was that it? Were we pregnant? Possibly the most momentous occasion in a couple's life and this was the best they could do for you? Why couldn't they make a stick that had bells or sirens on it? If birthday cards could play tunes for you, why couldn't a pregnancy-test stick? Once again, you paid your hard-earned money for all this technology and it invariably let you down at the critical moment. We looked at each other. A battle of wills as to who could go longer without saying anything. My wife spoke first — she always does. Usually last as well, come to think of it.

"That's a line, isn't it? I mean I can definitely see something. What do you think?"

Oh yes, here's a good idea, let's draw on my wealth of experience in taking pregnancy tests and clear this up once and for all. Naturally I merely thought this. What I actually said was:

"What do the instructions say? How much of a line do we need?"

This is one of the many situations in life that could easily be avoided by the remedy already referred to by my best friend as RTFM. So, my wife retrieved the said instructions from the bin and I waited for the judge's ruling.

(By the way, I hope you appreciate that I'm doing my best

to instill some tension and drama to this part of the story, even though from the title of the book, you quite obviously know the outcome. Bear with me.)

The ear-piercing scream was my first clue; the jumping up and down and flapping of arms in an idiotic fashion the second; and the enormous grin was the final giveaway. We were officially up the duff.

Elation and relief filled the room. The operations, the pain, the spoon, the hemorrhaging money, the waiting were all over. We had achieved our holy grail, and at the first attempt.

My Boy Scout training kicked in. I was prepared. I rushed to the fridge and grabbed the already chilled, suitably baby-sized, half-bottle of champagne and two glasses and took them back to the bedroom. I popped the cork with as much gusto and ceremony as possible. Within a few minutes of knowing we were pregnant, we were about to break the first rule and start boozing. My wife was having a drink to celebrate the sheer and unbridled joy at the fact she was pregnant. I just needed a drink.

As we chinked glasses and sipped champagne I was too wrapped up in the occasion to realize that we had actually created two new beings: The first of course being our own baby. The second, a creature as yet unknown to me, was The Pregnant Guy. I was about to become an unwitting accomplice on my wife's nine-month journey to Motherhood and all that would entail.

In the meantime, I decided to seize upon this opportunity, this historic moment of my wife's radiant happiness. After all, I was in no small way responsible for this joy. I intended to leverage my undoubtedly short-lived popularity into some long overdue sex. Besides, surely it was about time I gave my zipped-up scrotum a run out?

It took my wife less than a second to establish that the old guy and the newly created "Pregnant Guy" shared at least one unfortunate similarity.

LETTER TO DAD

Dad, I think I must have blacked out when you fired me from that cannon. There were so many of us leaving at the same time it was all a bit of a scramble and I may have been knocked over. Everyone was very nervous as we had no idea where we were going. I'm ok though, don't worry about me.

Anyway, when I woke up I discovered some of us had arrived at this fabulous resort. It looks foreign, Italian perhaps, as I think it's called something like Petri. I went for a swim in a huge circular pool. It's one of those fancy infinity pools with glass sides, where it looks like you can see forever. Very smart. It's quite shallow though and doesn't even appear to have a deep end. That's probably to help out some of the other guys, who don't seem to be able to swim very well at all. Some of them just go round in circles, chasing their tail.

Dad, I gotta tell you, there are some great looking eggs hanging out poolside and I don't mind saying I quite fancy my chances with one of them, she's really cute. Sure, there are some other sperm here also trying their luck, but they don't have as big a tail as I do. There are a couple of dodgy looking eggs lying around and the other boys can chat those two up. "Go ugly, early" is their best chance of success, if you ask me. Not for me though Dad, I'm aiming high.

So, I've been talking to this cute egg and we had a couple of drinks at the pool bar. She definitely has the X factor. I told her that was cool as my name is Y. We both laughed. It's almost as if we were made for each other. I'm giving it all the family charm and with a bit of effort, I think I can squeeze my way in there. Wish me luck, Dad. I think she could be the one.

Chapter 4

RETROSPECTIVE

IT SEEMED A SENSIBLE premise to me that the way my father brought me up was going to have a considerable bearing on how I would tackle the art of fatherhood. I considered this theory to be true regardless of whether someone had a fantastic relationship with their Dad, or a really tortured one. A person was left with two choices, but only one outcome.

If blessed with a great father-son bond, one would obviously want to try to emulate that with your own child as closely as possible. If someone was unfortunate enough to be brought up fighting constant conflict, it would naturally result in a firm intention to do everything completely at odds to their own upbringing. Either way, the net result was that your father still exerted a significant influence on the way you were likely to behave with your own child.

So I was drawn to ask myself the all-important questions. Did we have a good father/son relationship? What could I learn from my father in order to become a successful parent myself? How far would I need to go back through the family tree to find a decent parent? Do we have a family tree, or just a shrub, or worse. Are we merely the by-product of generations of bastard children through the ages?

These philosophical musings were going to need a bottle of wine. This whole baby experience already had my little brain hurting like it had been put onto the spin cycle, so I might as well take the necessary steps to ensure it would still throb in the morning.

As I'm sure many of us did in our youth, I often used to hear my father tell me how lucky I was to have him as a Dad, because his own father, my grandfather, was much more strict a disciplinarian to him than he ever was with me. To quote Monty Python: "We had it tough!" I had gotten off easy, apparently. Would that mean I too would be softer again on my own child? Or as with so many things genetic, would it perhaps skip a generation and make me the whip-cracking parent from hell?

I certainly hoped so. I considered being mean to your children and saying "no" as often as possible was a God-given privilege to parents and one of the few pleasures that made the entire ordeal of raising youngsters remotely tolerable. Just as a toddler could spit the pacifier out of the stroller as many times as you were silly enough to give it back, so too could a parent say no to almost anything with boundless enthusiasm, without even needing to provide a reason. For fathers especially, I believed it would be one of the particularly joyous experiences, because for years we had suffered a similar fate at the hands of our wives. We didn't even get the courtesy of the "headache" excuse any more, it was just a flat "no!"

But I digress. I can only say that I dread to think what my grandfather, who I never got to meet, must have been like, because I considered my Dad was himself a very stern character. I recalled all too well how he used to punish me for almost any and every indiscretion. It was only fair, therefore, that I fully intended to do likewise with my child. The experts say children need to know where the lines were. Well, my child would have more lines than the London Underground and suffer the same risk of electrocution should they ever be crossed.

My father had certainly served as a good example of that method. Yet although he was as hard as nails, he was an extremely fair man and always consistent. If he told me that action A would result in punishment B, I could rest assured that was exactly what would happen. It was perhaps a dubious honor, but I could at least say I always knew right where I stood and what I could expect. In poker parlance, he didn't bluff. My mother, on the other hand, bluffed constantly and folded almost as often.

"You do that one more time and I'm going to stop the car and you can walk home."

I was seven and we were still 20 miles away from our house. Even at that tender age, I was pretty confident that this was nothing to worry about, meaning I could merrily continue with whatever mischief I was up to with impunity. Sure enough, she never pulled the car over and I never had to wear out a pair of shoes walking home. And there were a thousand of these phrases for every occasion, all of which were treated with the same derision once I caught on to the hollowness of the warning. I used to love games, and this just seemed to be a really good one. As soon as I had worked out the rules and how to break them, my mother's ability as a figure of authority took a sharp nose dive.

There was of course one threat that did carry some weight:

"Do that again and I will tell your father."

That one worked. It was one of the easiest threats for her to fulfill and had the most devastating consequences. It was the parental equivalent of the nuclear deterrent.

Looking back, I actually developed a grudging respect for my father's steely resolve. As often as I would push his buttons and test his mettle, he was unwavering in doling out retribution, however inconvenient it may well have been for him. A lot of parents end up back-sliding on punishments as frankly, they were just as much of a nuisance for the parent as they were for the child. Parents were simply too tired and often couldn't be bothered. Punishing me was never too much trouble for my Dad.

I realize I'm starting to paint a picture of a miserable childhood with a mean-spirited father, when in fact that couldn't have been further from the truth. I consider that I had a great childhood. I was never spoiled, but I also never lacked anything that I actually needed, rather than wanted. I was just an average kid, with an average life, and I could have been a great deal worse off.

I would have to say that for the most part I remember myself as pretty easy going . So, just as I wondered whether I would be anything like my father as a parent, I certainly hoped my offspring would be cut from the same cloth as me as a child.

∞

My father and I still have an excellent relationship and one that has certainly improved with age. (Not a fate that would befall the wine, which I was knocking back pretty quickly.) A lawyer by trade, my Dad was by no means a frivolous man, so many of the activities that were associated with childhood, such as playing games and generally doing silly things that made a lot of noise and/or mess, did not appeal to him in the slightest.

"I never played with you kids," was his own summation. As I got older and moved toward his world, we were able to do more things together and became a lot closer. I was much more prepared to take time out to join in with his hobbies, largely because he wasn't going to participate in mine. I simply wanted to spend time with him.

Without question, our favourite pastime was going motor racing. When a younger man, he used to compete in some amateur meets and by the time I was six, he was taking me to the track with him. As soon as I was old enough to see over the dashboard while sitting on his lap, I learned how to steer the car; once my arms were long enough that I could reach the stick, I was changing the gears; the day the tips of my feet could finally stretch to the floor, I was stamping on the loud pedal and going as fast as I was allowed to.

From the safety of a race track, my Dad taught me how to drive — fast. He showed me how to "heel-and-toe," whereby your foot is on the brakes but also blipping the throttle to raise the revs as you change down through the gears before taking a corner at speed. He taught me how to go round a bend using the right line and hitting the apex. "Slow in, fast out," he would always say — the motto of many a Roman Catholic family.

On a rainy day, we sped down the straight and then slammed on the brakes. Once we finally screeched to a stop, he made me get out of the car (and of course, being my father, he really did make me get out) and trudge back to the point where we hit the skids. That walk made me understand just how long it takes to stop a car in the wet.

To teach me how to start on a hill, he was kind enough to put my watch behind the back wheel. If I got it wrong and let the car slide too far backward, I would need a new watch. Probably the hardest of all was when he placed an empty cardboard box on the hood and I had to bring the car to a complete stop without the box sliding off. Now think how much more relaxing it would be if every taxi driver was made to learn that trick.

On the open road, my job was chief scout and look out for the police patrol cars, as we were always speeding by a multiple of the limit. I had to spot the law before they saw us and it started getting expensive. That was back in the days when it was a fair fight between the two sides, before speed cameras and radar guns turned the tables in their favor.

Best of all were the conversations, or perhaps it would be more true to say the monologues. As we drove between home and the track and then home again, he would tell me countless stories of him and his friends and the things they got up to racing cars, either on the circuit or on the roads. However many trips we took, he always had another story to tell. Some bordered on incredulous, but it didn't matter.

Inside that car was a world where we were both doing something we enjoyed and we were doing it together. He instilled in me a love of cars that has never left me to this day. I watch Formula1 races with my wife and annoy the crap out of her by routinely pointing out things about 30 seconds before the commentator.

Otherwise, I can't say we did a great deal together. In my view there are two types of parents: Active and Passive. The active kind do everything with their kids: Sports, games, going to the park at weekends etc. Just generally being out and about and matching their children for boundless energy. The passives were probably the majority group, and my father was very definitely in that camp. I was sure the main reason he loved motor racing was because he could do it sitting down.

At weekends there were always chores to do, with me doing most of them if I wanted any pocket money. I would be outside mowing the lawn or washing the car, while he sat indoors, put his feet up and read the paper. It would seem another parental right was to use your children as a cheap form of labor. I was looking forward to exploiting that.

I could never claim that he ignored me though. The first time I got into the school rugby team, he unexpectedly turned up to watch the match. In the opening minutes, when I missed a tackle, he could be heard bellowing from the touchline.

"Come on you big Nancy, tackle him. Stop playing like a girl."

Call it sports psychology or dumb luck, but I certainly didn't want him shouting any further abuse at me, so my game improved drastically. From that moment on, no one got past me. Whether they were the biggest or the fastest, if they came anywhere within my reach with the ball, they were going down like a puppet with the strings cut. The fear of a considerably bigger opponent running straight at or through me was insignificant compared with the threat of more ridicule from the sidelines should I allow him to get past. Instantly, he made me a very effective rugby player. I'm sure the likes of Joe Montana and Johnny Wilkinson must have similar stories to tell of their childhood. Or maybe they just had talent.

Dad was even more vociferous in his support of my school work. His most draconian punishments were reserved for any failings in the field of academics, though I'm not actually sure this made any noticeable difference. Simply by looking at the results, it seemed pretty clear he didn't achieve the desired effect, although who knows how bad they might have been had he not done so. This could well have been because after receiving the discipline meted out to me by him, the paltry attempts of teachers to keep my nose buried in the study books and stamp out rebellion caused very little resistance to taking the wrong path.

If I had one single talent at school, it was to get away with the absolute minimum amount required for any given occasion. If a test had a pass mark of 50 percent, I would get 51. Should it be 70 percent, I would get 71. I was in the top set for everything and firmly rooted at the bottom of it.

"You wasted your education," was in fact how my father summed things up in his normal, blunt manner. I probably still owe him an apology for that — Sorry Dad — as I know he desperately wanted me to go on to higher learning.

Fathers always wish for their sons what they didn't have for themselves, and he had not been able to go to university. He studied for his law degree at night school while holding down a full-time job. He had to sit for all of his qualifications in his own time, yet passed them all with distinction. I only just managed to scrape through my exams, but with the type of grades that were only any good if I wanted to be a stripper, and certainly not ones likely to get me accepted to a decent college.

Our parents know the importance of a good education, but however hard he pressed me, I had no intention of wasting another three to four years in a classroom as I couldn't wait to get out into the big, wide world. He warned me repeatedly of the dangers of not having a qualification or a profession to fall back on. When I got fired from my job for the first time (and hopefully my last), it suddenly dawned on me he had a good point.

"When I was 16, I thought my parents knew nothing. When I was 21, I was amazed how much they'd picked up in the past five years" as Winston Churchill so aptly put it.

Having said all of this, I think I turned out ok. I managed to get another job, I'm writing a book, and I don't have a criminal record. I have even found a woman silly enough to marry me and have my child. Mind you, as far as the sex goes, she says I'm still doing the absolute minimum.

So the verdict is in. My Dad did a more than passable job of bringing me up. I gave him at least seven out of 10. This must put the odds in my favor that I too can be a successful parent. I even have the advantage of being at least a decade older than my father was when he took the plunge into parenthood, and the theory is that with age comes wisdom.

My Dad would probably give himself a lower mark, although his burden is to be judged by the standards of a different generation. For his day, he was a good father and did all the things he was expected to do. Namely, have a steady job so that you earned enough money to support your family; to be the peace-keeper and the trouble shooter.; and of course to maintain discipline. Fathers were not expected to spend "quality time" with their children — back then that was the mother's job. What today would be considered as bordering on negligence, in his day was deemed perfectly normal.

Of course this is only half the equation. As my father did a good job bringing me up and as I was from the same gene pool, albeit wallowing in the shallow end, I should have inherited some of his parenting abilities. By design though, the same should also be able to be said about my own child in relation to me. So the next question is: Was I a good child? What could I expect as I switched roles from son to father?

The first thing that surprised me was how absolutely delighted my father was to discover I was going to have a child. I never dreamed he would get such a kick out of being a grandparent. Perhaps this was another sign of what a good son I had been, that he was so looking forward to having a grandson? Perhaps not.

"I will enjoy every minute of you having a child, who hopefully will cause you as much misery and torment as you inflicted on me," he said. "I will laugh my head off every time you complain to me about how hard it is, how tired you are and how impossible your child is. Now you're going to know what it's like and what you put me through."

Perhaps I might have to reappraise that pass mark I awarded my Dad. His mean streak seemed to have reappeared with a vengeance. I may also have to reconsider my own report card as to how good a son I was, as there appeared to be some questions as to the validity of my self-imposed cherubic status.

I pressed him for details. Was I really that bad? What had I let myself in for? What was my child likely to do to me?

According to my father, as a young baby I didn't sleep. And that didn't mean I would only snooze for a couple of hours before waking again, or that I didn't want to take an afternoon nap from an early age. It meant that I literally did not close my eyes at all, which of course meant that neither did my parents. I was on the go all of the time, constantly demanding attention and wailing and screaming unless I got some.

Many a night my mother or father would pace the corridor, trying to get me to fall asleep. While in their arms, I was quite content and would be reasonably calm, which would lull them into a false sense of security and make them put me back in my cot. I would leave them a few minutes to let them get back to sleep, by which time I was bored with my surroundings and wanted another turn at that game where they carry me up and down the landing. So I would then attract their attention to let them know my desires.

It didn't take long before we were all at the doctor's office looking for medical remedies. The doctor (the very same one that brought me into the world) prescribed a mild sedative, which he said would put me to sleep for at least four hours. The result was not even four minutes. So, a few days later we were back at the clinic and he was doubling the dosage.

This too proved woefully ineffective and a week later my parents — sleep deprived and starting to think seriously about farming me out for adoption — were back again for stronger medicine. The doctor wrote a new prescription and informed them he was now giving me a potent enough sedative to knock out a 12-year-old child for up to eight hours. He said it was absolutely the strongest concoction I could safely be given.

My parents went away happy, thinking that the demon had been beaten. That night, they were actually able to get some sleep. Roughly 45 minutes uninterrupted. After that, I had fought through the fog induced by the drugs and had managed to claw myself back to consciousness.

Naturally, I now had twice as much energy as before, as I had just enjoyed this wonderfully long snooze. I was full of beans and ready to shout and scream all day long.

I was beginning to wonder whether we lived at the doctor's, or at least had a stake in the business. He was baffled by my SAS-style resistance to drugs and sleep, but undaunted. He reached for the prescription pad once more and started writing. My mother at least had some concern for my well-being, so she questioned the course of action we seemed to be taking.

"I thought you said we couldn't give him anything stronger than what we are already using," she reminded him.

"Don't worry," the doctor replied. "This isn't for him, it's for you. Someone needs to get some sleep, so if he's keeping you awake all night, you take the sleeping pill."

Thanks Doc. And thanks a lot Mom and Dad. So that night, I was left screaming my head off in my cot while they lay in a blissful, medically enhanced coma, no doubt with broad grins on their faces. I don't think it's an approach you will find in too many of the parenting books these days. And it was certainly not the definition of "controlled crying" as I understood it.

It was also a little worrying that some 40 years later my father seemed to remember every detail so clearly, and with such bitterness, that he wished the same misfortune inflicted on me.

He was equally delighted that I lived on a different continent, let alone country, so there would be no chance of the new parents appearing on granddad's doorstep to ask for help.

Without going into too many details, it transpired that there were many such stories about my being a nightmare to deal with. The so-called "terrible-twos" evidently lasted for about five years, during which time I managed to get up to as much mischief as possible on a regular basis.

How was it that our memories were so self-serving? Was it the same principle that allowed my eyesight to deceive me into genuinely believing that in my mirror, I was tall and handsome? Perhaps it was nature's own survival instinct? If we all remembered what horrors we were as children, we would never have any of our own and the world would be left to the cockroaches.

I was beginning to realize these were all questions I perhaps should have asked my father before I went through a scrotum-slashing operation to have my own child. Especially as it seemed the pain and suffering I went through for that proceedure was in fact a fairly accurate representation of what fatherhood was like.

And worse was still to come. Barely had I recovered from the barrage of abusive stories about me from my father — or as he would phrase it, stories about how abusive I was as a child — he made another comment. I imagine he thought it to be a conciliatory gesture and something of an olive branch. Instead, his words sent shivers down my spine and made the hair on my neck stand on end.

"Of course, your sister wasn't any better."

We men can be so insular. I was having a child, so I had thought about my own father and the relationship between us as the road-map to the bond with my offspring. Seeing it in the same light, I naturally presumed I too would have a son. All men want sons to play ball with, to watch sport with, to make and break things with, and of course to never go shopping with. But what if I did have a daughter? Would our relationship be similar to my sister's and my father's?

I had to tell my wife immediately there had been an awful mistake. I wanted my sperm back.

How far does this gene-pool theory go? Would my daughter be similar to my sister? My mother? Or would she naturally take after her own mother most of all? I had to hope for the latter.

My sister was the first born and like all eldest children, had to suffer experimental parenting from novice Mom and Dad. There was bound to be some trial and error, with the emphasis on error. Every mistake made with a first child surely had to benefit the second by the knowledge gleaned from those misfortunes. The eldest also had to be the pioneer for all who followed. They had to make the hard yards, and the younger siblings inevitably got an easier time of it.

In the same way that we all turn to look at car crashes, a morbid curiosity overcame me. I needed answers. I was compelled to not only ask my father about his recollections of his daughter's childhood, but also to politely enquire of my sister whether she felt inclined to relive a few memories of her own youth.

I think the mere suggestion almost put her in therapy. Her answer was blunt, unprintable, and definitely involved the phrases "retribution" and "legal action." So I shall delicately gloss over that particular side of our family history and move swiftly along. Suffice it to say that sometimes what is left unsaid speaks the loudest. Precious little use if you're trying to write a book, but there you go.

If my Marcel Marceau of a sister had actually volunteered anything, you would probably be amazed to discover we were brought up in the same household. For our respective views of proceedings were alarmingly different. From my perspective, it seemed we were pretty much treated the same, in as much as our parents always did what they thought was best for us. She would probably not agree. I suspect my sister's viewpoint would be that as soon as I appeared on the scene, I was the favored son. Frankly, I was equally happy with either definition.

To me it was a simple distinction. Boys were expected both to do things wrong and to do the wrong things. Fathers may even be secretly proud that their son was becoming a man and getting up to the same mischief he did when he was a lad. Boys were bound to get into trouble and it was not seen as a huge problem. In fact, it would be more of a worry if your son didn't.

However, a daughter was a very different proposition as far as fathers were concerned. She was meant to be perfect, a little princess who, despite being 16, was actually still only nine. She was absolutely not meant to get into any trouble at all, especially with the same types of boys that a father was secretly proud of.

Even if I couldn't glean any information from my sister about her childhood, there was certainly one area from where I could extract some hope.

My sister already had a daughter and was doing a marvelous job of raising her. I was convinced my wife and I would barely be able to cope between the two of us, yet my sister was doing everything with ease. If she could handle this parenting lark, then surely I could too. And as my niece had turned out to be such a delight, then shouldn't I be capable of producing a half-decent child?

So, my little daydream had taken me from fear and loathing through to resolute self belief that I had what it took to be a good parent, even if I also had what it took to produce a nightmare of a child. I was not quite sure how I had arrived at that conclusion, but I was mightily happy to have got there. Perhaps the now empty bottle of wine was responsible for both?

I was intent upon looking on the bright side. Pregnancy takes the best part of a year, so I still had plenty of time to hone my skills before the big day and the little bundle arrived. Surely I would almost certainly be an expert by then?

So that meant I would be left with plenty of excess hours to concentrate on the impending stage of pregnancy when my wife would turn into a raving nymphomaniac. I was still ever so patiently waiting for that.

LETTER TO DAD

Dad, I think I'm in deep trouble. I had a wild night with X, but when I woke up she was gone. I went out looking for her but couldn't find her anywhere. I've no idea what I said to upset her. I hope she's ok, as we were really growing on each other. In a funny way, I feel as if part of her is still with me.

Anyway, I managed to get myself lost so I decided to rest up for a bit. I had this weird dream that I was in some kind of huge water chute like at the Disneyland theme park. But now I think it wasn't a dream at all, because when I woke up I found myself in this really dark place. It seems like I'm down at the bottom of a well as it's quite damp. There are no windows and it has an echoey, hollow sound. It's nice and warm though, so I may just stick around for a bit and see if X turns up.

Some of the other guys that hooked up with eggs — I think there were about five of them — had said something about going off ice-skating. I didn't want to do that as I'm scared I might get frozen, but who knows, maybe they're better off? Perhaps the eggs they met were Canadian?

CHAPTER 5

PROTOTYPE

HAVING BEEN FORCED TO consider much more about my childhood than can be healthy for anybody, one thought from the far reaches of my memory did actually provide me with a modicum of optimism. Perhaps I didn't need to be quite so mortified about my wife's insistence that our child be born at home and I be present.

After all, I had been at a birth once before, and in all modesty, I think it would be fair to say that I had been the center of attention. What was even better was that I also had been born at home, so really, I could almost be considered an expert.

As my own memory of the momentous occasion was a little bit foggy, I decided to ask my parents for their faded recollections of my birth. I know they're pushing on a bit, but people say it's your short-term memory that goes first, while historical events remain crystal clear. Anyway, how could anyone forget an occasion like watching your child coming into the world? Surely it had to rank right up there with seeing the Super Bowl, World Series or Lord Stanley's Cup.

Apparently it all started innocently enough. My mother said she had always intended to have a homebirth. She would have done so for my elder sister, but the doctors of the day insisted that for a first child, she had to go to the hospital. As my sister's arrival evidently went very smoothly, it also confirmed to my mother the correctness of her initial belief that home, sweet homebirth was the best way to go. My father took an open-minded approach — it was the swinging sixties, after all.

"You don't argue against your pregnant wife."

Some 40 years later, how right he still was.

When pregnant with me two years after my sister, my mother attended classes that concentrated specifically on natural childbirth. My Dad didn't go, not necessarily because he didn't want to, but because back in the sixties that sort of thing just wasn't done. Having children was a woman's work and men were neither needed nor wanted. Some guys get all the luck.

Of course, that meant my Dad was fully at liberty to say that he desperately wanted to take the classes and support his wife, knowing that there was no chance it was ever likely to happen. In reality, he considered himself far too busy with real work and didn't want to have anything to do with it. I'm sure many of us men today would like to be able to get away with the same sentiment.

On the day of my arrival, everything started out just like another ordinary day. Both of them seemed to remember the early events with some degree of clarity. They had gone to the cinema that evening, although neither one can remember what movie they went to see.

The year was 1962 and it was a good one for Hollywood. The Oscar for best movie went to "Lawrence of Arabia," which also won in the Best Director category for David Lean. The Best Actor award went to Gregory Peck for "To Kill a Mocking Bird" and Best Actress to Anne Bancroft for "The Miracle Worker." Other nominated movies that year were "The Longest Day," "The Music Man," whatever that was, and "Mutiny on the Bounty."

My mother started having contractions during the show, and toward the end of the movie they started to get considerably stronger. She told my father they should leave immediately and that she needed to get home as soon as possible. It must have been an extremely good movie as he said no, he wanted to stay to see how it ended. Anyway, they were only 10 minutes from home, he argued. As the contractions started to bite, she concentrated more on her breathing than the movie, prompting a man in the row behind to ask her to be quiet. He said it sounded like they were having sex.

"That was nine months ago," my Dad hissed back. "Now we're suffering the consequences."

As the credits rolled, Mom and Dad quickly waddled home and prepared for the great event. Dad called the midwife to ask her to come over straight away. Having not attended any of the classes, he had no real idea what was going on, but even he could work out that things seemed to be happening at a faster pace.

There was no answer from the midwife. Being 1962, there was also no answering machine, no pager and no mobile phone with which to track her down. Another 15 minutes elapsed and he called again. Still no response.

"At this point I concede that I had become somewhat apprehensive that I might need to have a bigger role in the proceedings than I had ever intended," my father admitted to me in his typical lawyer-speak that could be used to deny any allegations of shortcomings at a later stage.

"Your father was absolutely petrified that he would have to deliver the baby himself," was how my mother preferred to describe his emotional state at the time, probably more truthfully.

While my father confessed that he had no idea what to do, he claimed he was not overly concerned as everyone else in the same situation had seemed to manage, so why should he be any different? History suggests otherwise, as after another fruitless phone call to the elusive midwife, he then immediately called the family doctor in a final plea for help. Fortunately, he only lived around the corner, and this being the by-gone era when doctors still actually made house calls, he said he would come straight over.

Once the doctor arrived both my parents agreed that everything settled down and an air of calmness returned to the house. That's because they also both agreed that they did not want my father in pole position when the baby came out. The doctor tried to keep my Dad busy, and therefore out of the way, by getting him to put on the kettle and make some tea. It was probably the most domestic thing he had ever done, but he couldn't refuse as he was under doctor's orders.

By all accounts, my actual birth was a breeze, as second children often are compared with the first. The labor was much quicker than my sister's had been. To his credit, my father stayed in the room the whole time to witness the event.

"Your mother was remarkably quiet," he recalled. "There were no screams of agony or anything. I made more noise cracking bad jokes and making stupid remarks. It was all pretty quick."

My mother concurred, saying that she had been concentrating so hard on her breathing exercises she never really thought about anything else. She was so much happier and more comfortable being at home rather than in the hospital, that she was much more relaxed.

"I can't truthfully say it hurt," my mother confessed (and I'll come back to that later.) "The only time I came close to screaming was at your father's awful jokes."

Once born, my father got a rush of male dominance and said that he wanted me to be circumcised. Not for any religious reasons, but simply because he had been. Thank God we had the doctor in attendance rather than the midwife, as he said no, it wasn't necessary, thus saving me from bodily mutilation. Just as well, as I really don't have enough to spare to start cutting pieces off.

I was then wrapped in a baby blanket, protecting my valuable bits from any harm. My father was asked if he wanted to hold his son, to which he responded like any new father would.

"Oh God, I'll break it."

And this from a man who already had a two-year-old daughter. I was also less than impressed by the reference to "it" rather than "him." He certainly was fully aware that I was a boy, as he had already suggested chopping off half my manhood.

So, apart from causing an involuntary shriveling in my nether regions, the story of my birth proved to me what I needed to know.

First and foremost, I had already survived one homebirth, so there was no earthly reason why I should not be able to manage another one.

Second, my father had not had the faintest idea what was going on from beginning to end, yet had managed to get through the entire experience without overly embarrassing himself. I could only hope to follow in the family footsteps.

LETTER TO DAD

Dad, sorry I haven't written for a while. I seem to have lost track of time. I feel as if I've been here for weeks, but it's hard to get any real information. It's sort of like living in a bubble, but at least it's very warm and cozy. I think I could be in a cell. Have I been arrested for the disappearance of X?

At first I thought I was alone, but recently I've noticed there are other cells around. In fact, every time I check, there seem to be more and more cells. First there were just two of them, then four, then eight, then as many as 16. The place is starting to get awfully busy. I've found out they're holding me in a place called Embryo. Can you come and bail me out please?

CHAPTER 6

BABY NAMES

EVOLUTION IS THE PROCESS of natural progression of the species. Generation by generation, animals make little improvements to the previous version, very much in the way that carmakers do. Most are extremely minor and caused by changes to the environment. Then, every once in a while, there's some kind of major breakthrough, such as walking on two legs or ABS brakes.

You may wonder then, why does it still take nine months to produce a baby?

Shouldn't we have advanced enough to have made that process a lot shorter by now? While nine months may rush by during a soccer or baseball season, it can seem an eternity for a pregnant couple. Why hasn't pregnancy evolved along with the rest of us? Sitting here in the 21st century, shouldn't we have honed the technique down to less than six months?

The most likely answer is because we need enough time to choose a *name* for our children. Animals don't bother, except in Disney. Otherwise, about the only baby in the litter to get a name is the last one, and that is referred to as the runt. Given the choice, it would probably just as soon go without the recognition.

History has proved that it takes the best part of a year to decide on a name for a child, so the baby might as well stay in the womb until we can come up with one. In fact, there are numerous instances that allude to the suspicion that nine months may actually not be long enough, and we should extend it to a year.

This is backed up by all the unfortunate children in the world who are called Junior, or something along the lines of Michael Wilson IV. Fine for Kings of England and all that, but a bit unimaginative for us normal folk, wouldn't you agree? It's an admission that after three-quarters of a year of almost constant discussion and debate, you simply couldn't come up with anything better.

But let's be honest, picking names is a very tricky business and certainly not one to be taken lightly. There are many hurdles to overcome and a lifetime of consequences to live with if you screw it up.

First of all there is the issue of relatives, particularly for younger parents, who tend to still have more of them around. Older relatives would like nothing better than to be immortalized by having a grandchild named after them. The first problem with this is that unless you also have a litter, there are more grandparents than there are babies to go around. Add to that the problem that choosing a name from one side of the family is automatically going to offend the other. Even using both won't work because you can't have a tie. One name has to come before the other. Someone is going to have to end up with second billing and they're not going to be happy.

Next is the problem that the older these relatives are, the worse their names tend to be. A lot of our forefathers evidently were even more inept at picking names than we are. Or perhaps they were just too busy with the industrial revolution and the occasional World War to give it too much thought. Who knows, maybe there just wasn't as much choice in those days.

I apologize unreservedly and in advance to anyone I am about to offend, but in this day and age , how can any parent with a conscience call their son Algernon, Bartholomew, Ebenezer and the like? Or their daughter Gertrude, Edna or Ethelred? What could any newborn child have done to their parents to deserve such a fate, however long and painful a labor the baby may have put the mother through? Or the agony of scrotum-ripping operations for Dad? Hey, there's an idea. Maybe if I have a son I can call him Scrotum, in case he forgets what I went through to create him?

There is of course one exception to this rule: If the said grandparent is absolutely loaded, then it is an acceptable and wise investment plan to name your child after them. Then your kid will leap-frog up the rankings in the will ahead of any older cousins with different names. If a child has to suffer a ridiculous name for a few years to inherit millions, then that's fair enough. He can change his name after the funeral if it's really that bad. If other kids at school tease your child for being called Humphrey or Willamina, then as soon as the inheritance kicks in you can simply buy the school and have the children responsible expelled.

The next battle you face still involves relatives. This time specifically your wife's family. It all goes back to the immortality issue and the growing reluctance of women to give up their birth name. Many women now insist any of their offspring must carry their own family name. To avoid the seeming pretension of a double-barreled surname, this means the wife's family name must now become the child's middle name, even though it often isn't a name at all.

That's how children are left scarred by names like Robert Gargoyle Smith, or Mary Snotty Jones. This can even include those with the most unfortunate surnames like Smelliebotom, whose friends suspect only got married in the first place to get rid of such an awful name.

Then there's the issue of pets. I don't mean that it's hard to name a pet, because it certainly isn't. Parents let their kids do it and wives even let their husbands make the decision, because it's so unimportant. If we're really honest, we don't care, and neither does the pet, which is unlikely to heed your command no matter what you call it. The only important rule is that your pet's name should in no way be offensive or inflammatory. You have to ensure you're not left standing in a crowded park at the weekend shouting "Loser" or "Slut" at the top of your voice to try to get your dog back. It's going to end in tears.

What I'm getting at is, apparently you can't give your child any name that has belonged to a pet of any close friend or relative. You may well want the name Max for your son. But if her Uncle Bob had a goldfish called Max that ended up getting flushed, then it's a non-starter for you. You may think Charlie is a great name, both for a boy or a girl. But if your wife used to have a cat called Charlie that got squashed by a car, then it's just not going to happen. It's almost as if by transferring the name, your child will also inherit the same sad fate. Apparently, your kid's destiny will be to escape through a window one day, chase a bird out into the street and get hit by a truck.

We are also faced with an explosion of what is considered acceptable as a name. Watch any game of American football or basketball; check out almost any descendant of someone in the entertainment industry, and we discover that anything goes. Instead of poring over a book of names with merely a few hundred standard variables, the world has opened up. The choice is now literally infinite, so it's going to take a lot longer to decide.

Geographic names are in vogue, whether it be a state such as Montana and Dakota, or a continent like Asia or Africa. The likes of Ohio and Antarctica haven't caught on yet, but give it time, the world is getting smaller. Countries and cities are also popular, like India or Sydney. (A hundred years ago, Sydney was a guy's name, but somehow the girls have kidnapped it. How did that happen?) David Beckham named his son Brooklyn, for no better reason than because that was where he was conceived. In our case, that would mean Pyrex for a boy, or Petri for a girl. But for many, choices of Conference Table, Seedy Motel, or Ford Pick-up leave a lot to be desired.

Despite this infinite choice, it's amazing how many families screw up. They either pick something that's simply atrocious, or fail to consider how the name may be shortened, lengthened or generally bastardized into something truly horrible. They also forget to consider what the name may represent when reduced to initials.

Just ask the Attric's son Jeremy, or the Prejudice family's daughter Rachel. What do you think Phillip Ness and Frank Uckwit are going to be called at school? How hard will life be for a boy if he is named Timothy Ian Tilton.

Of course, for some children it proves to be fairly academic. Whatever name they are actually given by their parents, it will seldom be used, except for official forms. The poor child will be stuck with a nickname forever. For the boys it seems to have a lot to do with carpentry. Chip, Chuck and Woody are all popular. For girls, they are unfortunately reduced to food groups. Honey, Sugar, Sweetie, Cookie, Muffin, or Cupcake. The only healthy one in the group is Apple, but I doubt young Ms. Paltrow is overly impressed.

ଓ୭

If you still don't believe the necessity for the lack of evolution in the length of pregnancy, let's look at what technological advances we have made. Take the ultrasound scan (for example). This amazing machine, now available in 3-D if you're in the Tom Cruise tax bracket, sends us a picture of the baby in the womb.

My stomach's big enough. I told the doctor I'd love to have a look and see what's in there. But as usual, us guys never get to play with the fun toys.

The picture is so clear that the doctor can tell you what sex your baby is. Now ask yourself: How does that help?

It's not for the doctor's benefit. He doesn't care what gender your baby is as it makes no difference to the delivery, or more importantly, the fee. Also, doctors almost never get the sex wrong when a baby is born, so they really don't need any advance warning as to what it's going to be. All those years of medical training kick in, they take a quick peak between the baby's legs and declare confidently, "It's a boy/girl." Almost a 100 percent record. Overly emotional fathers have been known to get it wrong, but doctors? No.

So what's the purpose of the ultrasound? That's right, you've guessed it. An early discovery of the gender is to help people who have no hope of choosing a name in the nine-month window. If you don't know the sex, then of course you have twice the problem as you need to pick two names, unless you choose something androgynous that will work for both. By knowing the sex, you can cut the problem in half straight away. Now you only have to agree on one name, and can pretend you would have been perfectly happy to have gone with your wife's choice if only it had been a boy instead of a girl, or vice-versa.

The only other benefit of knowing the sex is to avoid the fate of couples who become convinced of what they're going to have. All suggestions of girls' names are summarily dismissed because they just "know" they're going to have a boy. Often this is because of the result of some highly scientific test. Like hanging a wedding ring on a piece of string over their stomach, "asking" it what the sex is and seeing which way it swings! Almost foolproof, that one.

An erroneous result of one of these techniques can be traumatic for the child, as I imagine it may well have been for boys who were called Beverley, or any girl who got landed with the name Nigella. (Or perhaps even the first girl called Sydney?) The name had been chosen, everyone was happy, then suddenly the wrong sex baby comes out and ruins everything. Oh well, we'll just make the best of it and move on. You've got to have some sympathy for any of these kids who get lumbered with an inappropriate name. Who knows, perhaps just being called Adolf was enough to set him off.

A better way of telling the sex may be to take stock of what names you have on your short-list. If on the boy's side, you're both pretty much settled on David, while on the girl's side the list has only been narrowed down to a choice between Mary, Margot, Millie, Amanda and lastly Gertrude if grandma is still alive, then you can rest assured you're going to have a girl.

This game can go on for ages and may well be purposefully designed to help fritter away the many months of pregnancy. You're never short of conversation while you're trying to find a name for your baby. Every book or television show throws out potential candidates. Kramer was on my short list for a while for the same reason that George wasn't.

So it goes on. And so it should. It's our first major decision as a parent.

It may even be worth experimenting. Try shouting the proposed name at the top of your voice. Put some real venom into it, because you should know that this is the volume you're most likely to use when failing to get your child's attention. If you like, you can work up to it. Start out just with a stern tone in a steady voice, then gradually build up the volume, making the name more clipped each time, before finishing off with a real yell.

Some people prefer to start from a familiar abbreviation before going through the entire family name as represented on the birth certificate.

"Bob — Bobby —ROBERT —**Robert James Willcox!**"

But a name is an extremely important decision. One that your child will have to carry around for the rest of their life. At school, popularity can be determined by something as arbitrary as a name. Actors routinely change their names to something more fitting to the image they want to portray. Would John Wayne really have made it as a tough-guy cowboy had he kept the name Marion Morrison? Can a man singing songs at the piano in a sequined suit and an outrageous pair of glasses really pull it off with the name Reg Dwight?

For a long time it looked as if our child was going to have the very Italian-sounding name of Veto, as that was the most common suggestion from both of us.

"How about Molly? I like the name Molly, it just sounds

right," my wife would say over dinner.

"No, I veto that, too old-fashioned," I reply. "What about Nigel for a boy? I had a Godfather called Nigel."

"Veto."

"Why?"

"Because if you're vetoing Molly, then I'm vetoing Nigel. Do you like Nicholas?"

"Veto. You said your Dad's rottweiler was called Nicholas. How about Sasha?"

"Veto. What about Sebastian?"

"Not a fucking chance."

LETTER TO DAD

Dad, it must be a month or so and I have so much news. I broke out of that Embryo place and I need to hide out for a while until the coast is clear.

I'm holed up in a town called Fetus. I've taken a six-month lease on a womb. There was another couple after it as well, but I think they must have dropped out. It's not the biggest place you ever saw, but I got a cheap deal and I'm sure it will grow on me. I'm not going to bother with any decorating, even though it's a bit dark. I think this place may have mold as well because the walls seem to be moist. I'm guessing it's also very close to a construction site as I can hear this constant thumping noise. It slows down at night, but they never seem to stop working.

The landlord is pretty strict. He said that he didn't like tenants hanging around too long and would evict me once my time was up. In fact, he hinted that if he really didn't like me, he knew some people who could remove me by force, so I'd better be on my best behavior.

CHAPTER 7

TRAINING

M Y WIFE HAD FOUND us a new hobby for the weekends. Whenever we had some free time available, (which we often did after I have been made to cancel whatever it was I had originally planned to do) we went to visit friends. But of course being that we were pregnant, it wasn't that simple or straightforward. These were not just any old friends, but a very specific group that could cater to our particular needs.

These were friends who had recently had their own children. In fact, seeing them was merely a shallow pretense, because it was only really their baby that we were interested in. Or to be even more precise, that my wife was interested in, as I was still at the stage of manhood ruled by the motto "Children should be neither seen nor heard, nor even let out of their room unless it's an emergency."

Whenever we had visited similar couples in the past, there had always been an extremely quick and mutually agreed-upon splitting up of the sexes. The girls would go one way and talk babies; the guys would rush off in the opposite direction and talk sports. It was a tried-and-tested technique and it worked surprisingly well for all involved. She was talking about the subject she loved the most to other people who were actually interested and prepared to listen; I was being totally ignored by my wife and therefore not getting into any trouble — sometimes for as long as two or three hours.

Sadly, that was to be no more. Now a visit to a friend's house was the adult version of summer school. Idiot-Dad-in-Training was being brought round to get some practice handling a real-life baby.

In all of this, it was the baby you really had to feel sorry for. The poor little thing had even less say in the matter than I did. Usually not even a year old, it was only just getting to grips with life in general and had finally learned not to cry every time one of those two huge heads appeared in front of its face making scary gurgling noises and blocking out the light. Having lived through the constant fear that it was going to be eaten alive by one of the giant craniums, now suddenly, it was going to have to endure being a human experiment.

Most of my wife's friends had previously had the wisdom not to even leave me alone in the same room with their baby for fear of the repercussions. But it seemed the simple fact of my wife being pregnant had granted me with instant expertise in child handling. It made no sense to me at all and was the type of logic only other women could possibly understand. The only male equivalent that I could compare it to was the belief among fat, balding men in their forties that buying a Porsche 911 convertible made them young, handsome and positively irresistible to women.

With the same speed that I used to get offered a cold beer, I was now presented with the unfortunate baby. It was tough to know which one of us was more uncomfortable with the situation. All the other adults present looked on with keen interest to see which of the two of us would be the first to wet themselves. I was convinced some parents were even mean enough to put something in their child's diaper before handing it to me, as any baby in my grasp immediately started squirming and writhing like someone in a 70's disco.

My first tactical move was to sit down — anywhere, on anything. In one swift move I had reduced the drop-zone by about 50 percent, also significantly lowering the prospect of brain damage to mere bruising and a slight headache. At least if I could perch junior on a knee, I might be able to provide some stability and get the little bugger under control. Occasionally, this was greeted by a nod of approval from the true parent. If I was really lucky, there might even be a wink in my wife's direction, almost like I was getting a silent vote of support: "You see, your husband is not the complete moron you said he was after all."

That was usually my high point though, and things would quickly go downhill from there. After all, what can you actually do with a 10-month old kid? Conversation was severely limited to gurgling noises; he almost certainly went to bed before last night's game; and although overweight, my upper torso provided neither the entertainment nor the nourishment that his mother's did. Luckily, I was born with a silly face, so no effort required there to provide something to laugh at. Like most men, I jiggle my leg whenever I sit down, so at least that was offering some form of activity and making it look like I was actually taking an interest in the little rascal.

It was this feeling of wellbeing that normally started the trouble. Before I knew it, distractions were breaking my concentration. Real Dad had finally brought me that cold beer. I felt happier than a performing seal getting his first fish after completing a trick. So now I was down to just one hand holding onto the bambino. Faint memories of the first time I tried to ride my bicycle without using the handlebars flashed across my subconscious, but I failed to heed the warning signs.

As we all learned in physics class, all science teachers are weird, but they taught us that light travels faster than sound. So that meant that before I had heard the thud, I had seen the look of absolute horror on the faces of my panel of parental judges. Still, only being Dad-in-Training, I instantly and unfortunately worried that I had fallen foul of the ultimate sin of spilling my beer. So first I looked in that direction to assess the situation. Needless to say, I hadn't wasted a drop, but now that I had looked at it, naturally I took a quick slurp. This caused a gasp from the gallery, and even worse, I think there was a tiny little squeak from Real Mom. That was the cue for me to realize that my leg was moving with much more freedom than it had been just a minute ago.

My beer-free hand, although still cupped to hold a small child, was now also baby free. Junior was on the floor. My initial hope that he had climbed down my trouser-leg in an amazing early feat of dexterity was quickly quashed by the fact that he was face-down on the ground, immobile. My ignorance of all things baby-related allowed me another fleeting glimpse of redemption. Even though he was sucking the carpet, he wasn't actually crying. Perhaps I could still get away with this?

Of course those people who already have kids know the answer. Babies' brains, very much in the formative stages, take a while to come to decisions, as they don't have an awful lot of experience to draw from. In a situation such as this, the process went roughly as follows:

"Hey, I'm bouncing. This is fun. I've done this before. Wow! I'm flying. I think I've done this before as well, but it felt different because my Daddy keeps hold of me. This is better. Look, here comes the carp – Oooff.

"It's gone dark. Where am I? Why is my heart in my nose and why is it beating so fast? It's hot. I'm not breathing. My nose hurts. I need to tell the big people my nose hurts. How do I do that again? Oh yes. Deep breath, and WAAAAAAAAAAAAH-HHHHHH."

Mere Dad-in-Training I may be, but that was a sound I recognized and understood. It meant today's lesson was over. Another test had been failed and I just knew there was going to be extra homework. Real Mom was looking at me like I was a serial killer. My wife was looking at me like I was the dog that just crapped on the carpet. My guess was we would be leaving any minute now. Our welcome had worn thinner than the skin on junior's little nose.

Not to worry, we were off to see Ted and Alice next. Their

child was a couple of months older than this one. Perhaps I should sit on the floor at their house. Live and learn. By the time my own baby was born, maybe I wouldn't need a warning label any more. I just hoped we would still have some friends left.

I also for once hoped that this wasn't the day my wife's nymphomania phase kicked in, as she had given me a look so cold I expected a light to come on when she opened her mouth.

There was another source of education available to me, and let's face it, when I became "The Pregnant Guy," I was a blank piece of paper as far as knowledge and understanding of the topic were concerned. That was probably because if I had known a little bit more about the subject I would never have allowed myself to get into this situation in the first place.

The benefit of this form of education was that it came straight to me, free of charge, and I didn't have to lift a finger to get it. The downside was the incredible quantity of the information I received and the very questionable nature of its merit.

One of the first things I had thought when I was told I was going to be a father was what an incredibly personal experience it was all going to be. After all, I was helping to bring a miniature version of myself into the world. What could be more personal than that? My first lesson this free-education service revealed to me turned out to be the total misconception of my original belief.

Lesson number one was that I quickly discovered that my situation was not something personal, but rather something communal that had to be shared with everyone else. Or to be more precise, something that everyone else wanted to share with me. As soon as the world at large discovered that I was not only Pregnant Guy but even better than that, I was a novice Pregnant Guy, my education started. I instantly had to be prepared for a barrage of information from anyone who had ever had a child, anybody who knew someone else who had had a child, or anyone who was further along than me in the process of having a child.

These people reveled in the fact that I obviously knew practically nothing about having a baby, while they apparently knew absolutely everything, or possibly slightly more than that. No matter if I was shy, for I had no need to actually ask for assistance. These caring people would volunteer to impart their wisdom readily and repeatedly, as if the very success or failure of my own pregnancy depended on it. So God forbid they should leave out a single solitary fact that might prove vital, especially as they were probably the only soul on the planet that knew this particular kernel of knowledge.

These kind souls could basically be sorted into two categories, which, without meaning to generalize or be sexist, could also roughly be split by gender.

The first group, an honor I shall bestow on the women, imparted education on the basis of personal experience. Their belief was that my child's birth, rather than being in any way unique, was going to be almost identical to their own. So the best way to prepare me for this eventuality was to tell me exactly what happened to them during their pregnancy and childbirth: Step by step, week by week, month by month, and contraction by every individual contraction.

Often this was done with a degree of detail that was scarily open, honest and blunt, leaving me knowing considerably more about my new tutor's inner workings than I could ever possibly have wanted. Women who I had not met often enough to remember their names (which admittedly for me could still be three of four times) would happily tell me things I considered only their doctor or perhaps their priest should know.

Again, the only real advantage of this schooling was the total lack of effort required on my part. The only muscles I used were my ears, and perhaps the occasional neck movement to denote that I was still both awake and listening. Questions were asked periodically, but they were largely rhetorical and anything more than the briefest hesitation on my part was greeted by the metaphorical sound of a slamming window as I missed my opportunity to speak, thus allowing her to get another lungful of air and soldier on.

"Has your wife's appetite changed?"

(Momentary pause prompted by the absurdity of the question — or maybe this is where the phrase "pregnant pause" came from. Who knows?)

"Well it will. I'm surprised it hasn't already. How many months is she?"

(No answer required, expected or wanted.)

"I had by that stage, and let me tell you," yadda, yadda, yadda and she was off again, while I wondered whether the story of her pregnancy was actually going to take the full nine months to recount. Some of the things she had told me about what I could expect to happen to my poor wife's body (because that was what had happened to hers) were frighteningly graphic. I had to be on my guard at this point because I was scared she might even have photos. And all this was just about the pregnancy. I still had the grand finale to get through.

The hardest part of all this was the total selflessness with which it was all done, which made it almost impossible to reject without seeming extremely ungrateful. These people genuinely thought they were doing me a huge favor by sharing their birth experience with me, so that I would be fully forewarned and fore-armed when my time came. They were giving me the essential information that I couldn't possibly have known, having not had the benefit of their experience. When they eventually let me escape, they considered that they left me a wiser man.

However, one thing these particular women seemed to have conveniently erased from their own memories was how incredibly hormonal and emotional pregnant women were. Had they recalled that fact, they would have realized my currently pregnant wife, duly sensitive and illogical, would heap monumental amounts of grief on me for having spent the past however long talking to another woman.

"Who was that you were talking to for so long?" My wife probably knew the said woman a lot better than I did, but she would start with this accusatory question anyway. "You find her attractive don't you?"

Perhaps my wife had already had a conversation with this woman, as she already seemed to have picked up her art of rhetorical questions. Not that I would ever have been stupid enough to even consider trying to reply to that question, which as all men know, has no correct answer.

"Well, you obviously don't find me attractive any more as you spend your whole time talking with other women. I'm just fat and ugly."

Another hand grenade to deal with. This one wasn't even a question, but equally fraught with danger, just the same. Hesitate too long and let the fuse burn down and it would blow up in my face. My only chance was to try to smother it.

"You look radiant, my love."

I don't know who invented the word radiant, but Pregnant Guys the world over owed that person an enormous debt of gratitude. It seemed to be the permanent "Get-Out-of-Jail-Free Card." I was just worried that I was wearing it out too quickly. By month four or five of the pregnancy I was going to have to come up with something new. Where was my lesson for that situation?

The second group, who by a process of elimination must be the men, were similar in that they too wanted to impart the experiences learned from becoming a father. The difference was that it came very much in the form of a warning, rather than constructive advice.

Fellow men wanted to tell me, in equally gory detail, about all of the horrible, revolting, nasty things I was likely to suffer as a pregnant guy. No sugar-coating, no sympathy. This was not a romantic movie they were recounting, but a hard-hitting documentary. This group of men delighted in telling me about every mistake I would make, every horror I would have to face, every torture I would undoubtedly suffer.

And it was not preventative medicine. I was not being told as a warning to save me from a similar fate. Oh no. I was being told as a prophecy of my future, a vision of my doom from which there was no escape. I was on the Yellow Brick Road of pregnancy, my wife was the Wicked Witch of the West and I was the lion with no courage.

They told me because they *wanted* me to suffer as they had suffered, perhaps even more than they did because I was now going to know it was coming, because they told me it was coming. They wanted me to join their ranks and were simply telling me about the many initiation ceremonies I would have to endure to become a member.

The evil was compounded to satanic proportions because these men — my friends until now — had never uttered a word of this to me *before* I became a Pregnant Guy. No parent ever tells a non parent the truth about having a baby. They all wheel out the platitudes and suck you into the trap.

"Best day of my life, the day Junior was born. I'm a totally different man now. I've grown. I just want to spend all my time with him. You can't believe you can love someone as much as you do your own child. You gotta have kids."

Actual translation, once you are about to have your own child and there's no turning back:

"The last day of my former life. I'm a mere shell of the man I once was. I'm stuck with this kid the entire time and I haven't played golf in months. Welcome to the club."

Only once in the club does the truth come out. Knowing nods and winks are passed between these men as they report their humiliations, such as the trips to the fertility clinic and the pre-natal classes. One friend told me his wife getting pregnant proved to be a great boost to his career as he suddenly didn't mind working late at the office every night.

These so called friends should have been giving me condoms and saving me from this peril, but instead they waited until I had passed the point of no return and then unleashed the full fury of the truth upon me.

Of course almost none of these stories could be classed as information I could actually use, but it certainly was educational. Pregnancy was a nine-month sentence with no chance of parole. Women may be the ones that do the heavy lifting, but it seemed evident that every opportunity was taken for their men to share a lot of the burden one way or the other — and all of the blame.

With the utmost trepidation, I plucked up the courage to ask the one question that was the small speck of light at the end of the pregnancy tunnel. Was it indeed true that pregnant women went through a period of relative nymphomania and wanted sex *all* the time? Could men find an oasis in the pregnancy desert? While not completely unheard of, it was beginning to seem as if this story had more than an element of urban legend to it. Those few who said they had seen the promised land suggested I would need a very open interpretation of the term nymphomaniac. I assured them that just participation would probably clinch it for me.

Still, with the dressing-down I had just received from my wife for talking to a non-pregnant woman for more than a few minutes, I knew it wouldn't be this weekend.

Was it just me or were the days getting longer?

LETTER TO DAD

Hi Dad, how long has it been? Too long, I know. Sorry about that. But you'll forgive me after you hear the amazing news I have to tell you. You're going to be so proud.

I have hands and feet! Isn't that great? Everything is where it should be I think; five fingers on each hand and five toes per foot. Is that right? Which one is the rude finger and why is it called the rude finger? They're all pretty small though. I don't think I'm going to be playing the piano or kicking a ball anytime soon. Still, at least I can wave.

Dad, can I ask a personal question? Please don't get angry with me if it's a stupid one. After all, I'm not exactly dealing from a full deck yet. Are we some kind of fish? I only ask because my fingers and toes seem to be stuck together. I don't mean I'm bent double holding my feet, but if it got cold I'd have to wear mittens instead of gloves, if you know what I mean. I noticed at the Petri resort that some of the other guys looked a bit like tadpoles, so you can understand my concern. It would also explain my affinity for water.

CHAPTER 8

VORTEX OF EVIL

(Sort of)

I N MARRIED LIFE, THERE is no end of things that
can and will frighten the living daylights out of the unsuspecting Pregnant Guy. I discovered that one of the scariest of
them all was probably the one that you would have expected
the least — which of course was what made it all the more
terrifying.

You can read books; you can talk to friends who have been
through the process; you can take medical advice; heck, you
can even take medication, but nothing can really prepare you
for the horror that awaits you. For this was to be an event that
would leave an indelible scar on my psyche for the rest of my
living days.

I had been lulled into a false sense of security by the belief
that nothing worse *could* happen to me after having had my
scrotum cut open. Surely I had already made the ultimate
sacrifice to create this baby? Could I now not walk tall, albeit
a bit bow-legged, in the knowledge I had already survived
and overcome the greatest evil known to Mankind? Did I

not deserve to now live free of fear and further retribution? It would transpire that the answer to those questions was a resounding: No, I did not.

Like most tragedies in life, it happened on a typical Saturday afternoon when the world seemed at peace and there was no portent of danger. One minute everything was as it should be. Sixty seconds later, the world as I knew it had ended. And I was only just getting used to this new world after the last one disappeared into a thin blue line on a stick. Without warning, I was sucked into a living hell where pain and suffering knew no boundaries. I had entered the Mothercare shop.

And before I get sued for what few pennies I have, please note that I am simply using Mothercare as the most well-known example of the genre that is shops for baby accessories. (Please also note that I did not use the word "necessities" as that could not be further from the truth.) If anything they should be taking it as a compliment. I could just as easily have referred to any store that caters to expectant and new mothers. So please, Mothercare Board of Directors and especially the Legal Department, take it as a mark of respect and a token of your undoubted success in this field.

So where was I? Ah yes. If there is a vortex between the worlds of good and evil, Mothercare is it. This is the spot, rather than Sunnydale, where Buffy and her cohorts are needed to do some serious slaying. Hercules was only able to complete his 12 tasks because one of them wasn't going to Mothercare. James Bond only managed to repeatedly save the world from disaster because he had all his gadgets made for

him by Q, so he didn't have to go down to the local Mothercare store to buy them.

Not surprisingly, baby shops are very much an unknown
world as far as most men are concerned, similar to the Yukon,
or the laundry. We have heard of them, we do know they exist,
but we have absolutely no idea what goes on there and even
less intention of finding out.

So what was such a big deal? You may ask. Men get dragged
to women's shops all the time. Well, our wallets do, but as we
usually try to stay attached to them, we tend to get taken along
for the ride. We have visited countless shoe shops, numerous
clothing stores, the occasional supermarket and if we're really
unlucky, some form of jewelry store. We follow obediently,
nodding dejectedly at any other fellow males we see that are
caught in a similar predicament. Misery loves company. We
just hope we can get home before the game starts.

But if ever our pre-pregnant wives have made a visit to
Mothercare, then it was a secret mission from which men were
thankfully excluded. No surprise really, because if your not-
pregnant wife ever came home with a bunch of shopping bags
from Mothercare, it was surely going to provoke a conversation, and quite possibly a seizure.

So, having barely survived to tell the tale and spread the
warning, what exactly am I going on about? In a nutshell,
it's the fact that as soon as my wife walked into the baby
store, some strange power took control of her faculties and she
wanted to buy every single item that was for sale. There was
no question the force was with her and it was very definitely

from the dark side. Other women seemed to be possessed by the same affliction. There didn't even need to be a requirement for any of them to actually *be* pregnant for this condition to overpower them.

Logic was checked at the door. Pregnant women could easily end up buying an outfit that was actually intended for a two-year old, simply because "it's so adorable." Women who have had a boy still wanted to buy pretty little baby dresses. And everyone apparently had to buy a teddy-bear before they were allowed to leave the premises. It must have been written somewhere in the small print.

First of all, these shops should have security guards on the door, to act as a very necessary warning that you were about to enter an exceedingly dangerous place. Before being allowed admittance, all men should be thoroughly frisked to ensure that they were in the possession of at least one gold credit card. Anyone with less was just not going to make it out of there alive.

Secondly, there should be trained staff on hand for instant medical check-ups. The more frail amongst us guys could easily have a heart-attack, stroke, go into shock, or at a minimum feel extremely weak and need to sit down. Frankly, I was surprised to hear that they had not been sued themselves at some point.

When I first innocently entered the store I was confronted by an array of baby shoes. Nothing is more irresistible to even the most heartless among us than teeny-tiny little pairs of shoes. They even look fantastic just as ornaments, let alone actually as functional items of footwear. Almost instantly, they break the spine of resistance in all but the most courageous of men. And that certainly wasn't a definition that had been used about me in some time.

Baby shoes are the retail equivalent of a sucker punch. Naturally, within the enormous selection, there will be pairs of miniature sneakers or microscopically sized football boots and golf shoes to suck in the jocks and get them thinking they can dress Junior in their own image. For the women, it's an instant "Advance to GO and spend $200 dollars."

These Mothercare people are no fools. Women are barely able to resist buying themselves shoes they don't need, aren't comfortable, or worse, didn't even fit properly, so there was no chance they would be capable of using restraint when buying footwear for their child.

Pregnant women will buy both pink and blue pairs of shoes because they don't yet know what sex their child will be. Women are also completely preconditioned to paying quite ridiculous sums of money for shoes they will rarely wear, so it is an easy starting point to get them to spend freely when buying the very first pieces of footwear for a baby.

Now here was the *really* clever part, if you just thought about it for a minute. Babies can't even walk before they are about one year old, so why would they possibly need a pair of shoes? If a pet shop sold waterproof sandals for goldfish, however stylish, would you buy them?

Even after they are a year or two old, have you ever observed a child's reaction to actually wearing a pair of shoes? Did they look down at their feet and give an appreciative nod that said, "Hey, cool shoes. Thanks Dad." No, they did not. You might want to think they did, but they didn't.

The first chance they got, the little brats took them off and threw them somewhere where they hoped you would never be able to find them again. As they couldn't yet throw very far, that usually didn't work very well, so the offending articles promptly returned to be re-attached. Step two was the child then chucked an absolute hissy-fit when anyone tried to put the shoes back on. So began the struggle to get them wearing the said footwear. You try to hold them down, while they wriggle worse than a greased pig. And, being more flexible than soggy fettuccini, they appear able to keep their feet somewhere you can't seem to get hold of them.

By the time you had won the battle (minimum duration, seven minutes) and the child was finally wearing its shoes, it was then too tired to actually walk anywhere and needed to be carried. So, once again, the shoes were redundant, except to improve the baby's ability to kick you in sensitive areas or transfer dirt onto your clothing. But hey, didn't they just look great?

Once we had broken the ice with the shoes, it was a piece of cake to move on to the main clothing department and go completely nuts. As all women have read in their shopping bible, shoes need outfits to match. These baby-store people were so confident, they were happy to take a slight risk here by separating baby clothes into various age groups, usually at intervals of about three months. This should of course have acted as a warning to prospective shoppers that babies grow so fast that every dozen weeks or so, they have moved beyond one set of clothes and need the next size up.

The brilliance here is taking advantage of one of the recurrent themes of my book. Pregnant women lose almost all cognitive skills of decision-making. Most men, uninitiated as they are in all things birth-related, would still have a strong instinct that the correct clothing size for a baby that had not even been born yet was the one that started at zero. That was all we needed to get going. This is then followed by a sequential move up through the numbers, with a couple of items in each category sufficient to keep baby dressed until we get to the next size up. Job well done. Still time for a beer.

Not so the women. What if the baby is born really big? It might already be a 0.5 or a 0.7 and would almost certainly be too large for a zero. So, to be safe, we would need the zero *and* the one. What if the baby doesn't grow for say, the first year? Well, we had better buy enough zeros to last at least 18 months just in case. You can never be too careful.

Alternatively, what if the baby grows like a weed in mid-summer? It could be heading out of one-city and approaching two-ville before we knew it. The only solution was therefore to buy the complete range on offer.

A brief nod here must be given to the Mothercare management, who obviously went to a conference in Las Vegas at some point. For they had cottoned onto the wisdom of stacking the odds in their own favor to give the house an edge. Yes, baby clothes did indeed start at zero, but let us not forget about those little decimal places. We didn't just have one zero, we also had double-zero and even triple-zero. Kind of like xxx-large, but in reverse. Three sizes in one, for a week-by-week wardrobe as your child develops. These infant sizes could almost be described as disposable clothing. Their shelf-life was so short they would probably only be worn once before being discarded as too small. Was their no end to their evil cunning?

More importantly, it was a conundrum that the vast majority of pregnant woman were not going to come even close to solving. They quickly deduced that the most effective solution is bulk buying of an indiscriminate nature. Every size, in every colour should cover it. The obvious result of this was some unfortunate purchases that, in a rare moment of clarity, these Moms might actually concede served no visible purpose and would never get worn. The next conclusion was unfortunately another trip to the store to return the offending items and buy numerous replacements — and another two pairs of little shoes.

Baby shops were more addictive than heroin and equally expensive. They needed to carry a health warning.

And don't think you were anywhere close to finished after the clothes racks. We were also going to need all the accessory items. Little hats and baseball caps were everywhere.

This was evidently another ploy to hook the unsuspecting Dad, who of course was trying to have his son dressed to look like his own little version of "Mini-Me." Not groovy baby, no. They may well both even need a baseball cap to cover the same bald spot. It also had the downside of allowing the women an extra "free" purchase, as they considered buying something that their husband would like didn't actually count. In fact, it could almost be seen as a credit against another purchase.

By the way, for those of you who don't yet know the painful truth, hats rank right up there with shoes as appendages that are almost instantly discarded. Worse, they are even easier for the child to dispense with as they are not so well attached as a pair of shoes. The stealth with which a baby can drop their hat over the side of the stroller, making you walk 200 yards back down the street to find it, has to be seen to be believed. It was probably the first skill David Copperfield learned on his way to being a superstar at disappearing tricks. It is also a game they *never* tire of playing.

Next we get to toy division. The cuddlier, the better. Teddy Bears ranged from little miniature teddies that seemed small enough for a toddler to choke on, to life-size monsters that would surely scare the crap out of any baby. Were we actually meant to put these things in their crib, so it was the first thing they saw when they opened their little eyes? Some of them were so big there would have been no room for anything else. They could have toppled over and trapped the poor baby underneath, with its screams for help muffled by mounds of synthetic, chemically treated fur.

If you didn't like teddy bears, there was no need to worry at all. There was also a literal Noah's Ark of other animals to choose from.

It's ironic that we spend all of a child's formative years

surrounding them with stuffed pets, until they get old enough for us to tell them how dangerous animals are and that they must stay away from them. And if a certain breed of creature wasn't dangerous, well that kind we would almost certainly kill, cook and eat.

Eventually, I got closer to the cashier and started to believe I might actually escape within the next thousand dollars. It was then that my flagging energy was given a shot in the arm and I stumbled upon something to stop me from going completely out of my mind. Having been dragged from section to section seeing my life savings rapidly diminish, finally I arrived at an oasis. All Hail the Vehicular Department.

At last there was an area for us "Pregnant Guys." Just as well, as I had started to worry that my feminine side was creeping a bit too far over the boundary. Suddenly I was lost in a world of strollers and buggies. There were wheels everywhere. Everything from little three-wheelers to eight-wheeler big-boys. Now we were talking.

I kicked the tires; tested the brakes; played with all the knobs and buttons to see what they did; kept playing with all the knobs and buttons even though I couldn't work out what most of them did; took off various pieces to inspect the inner workings more closely; put the pieces on the floor and moved on quickly to the next stroller because I couldn't seem to reattach those bits back onto the vehicle; and best of all, I took that puppy for a spin round the store to see how it handled in tight, high-traffic situations.

It was in the midst of this heady euphoria I discovered that the expression "vehicular" was a bit too close for comfort, because at these prices, it was almost like I was paying for a car. Even the names were familiar. For the motor racing enthusiast, there was a brand called Maclaren, which seemed to come with a similar Formula 1 price-tag. But it had the sleek, aerodynamic looks and a suitable amount of technology. Then there was a multitude of Italian-sounding names such as Graco, Chicco and the like, which surely were faster than your average stroller, even if they were likely to rust and have a terrible second-hand value. And the choice was simply unbelievable. Who would have thought there could be such variety in something as functional as a stroller. But it transpired that if you wanted one with a drink holder and an ash-tray, then you could have it.

For those of us who really liked gadgets, there was also a hybrid version that was both a stroller and a car seat rolled into one. Most men in the store could now show their superior ability at dismantling things and their total incapability in putting them back together again. If you took one of these hybrids out for the day and forgot to bring the manual, your baby may have to stay strapped in until it was old enough to work out how to escape on his own.

These hybrids were so versatile, and looked so sensible, you didn't even notice that it actually cost more than buying a car seat and a stroller separately. But who cared, it was cool.

There was even a jogging stroller, made by someone who quite obviously has never had children. Most new parents barely have the energy to push a stroller downhill, let alone go running with one. But it alluded to that fanciful dream many people mistakenly share that having a child was not going to change their lives.

The theory went like this: Our baby is going to learn to live life on our schedule, rather than force us to change everything to suit its needs. We will simply keep doing what we have always done, and will just include the baby in our activities. The most important thing is a routine, so we will simply introduce the baby to our routine and carry on as normal.

I can't claim to be an expert, but seeing how much our prior life and habits have been completely thrown out the window just by my wife being pregnant, let alone actually having a baby to deal with, I'm guessing that theory will be about as successful as a chocolate teapot. For once, there was going to be something my wife and I were instantly going to agree on: Cross the jogging stroller off the list, please.

Here's another clue for you. Babies don't have schedules or routines. They can't even tell the time. They do what they want, whenever they want, with the only degree of certainty being that most of these events will happen at the most inopportune times in the most public places.

But I digress, so let's reverse to the stroller department, making beeping noises as we go. Alongside the fantasy-jogger in the Sports Utility Vehicle section, there was also a kind of trailer to fix on to the back of your bicycle to take baby on those longer journeys.

Great idea Mr. Designer. I shall cycle along the road and keep my precious new baby in a ground-level capsule that no driver in a car, let alone a pick-up truck, is going to see until they ask "what did I just hit?" Even if we avoided a collision, the baby would probably die of carbon-monoxide poisoning as it was dragged along the road at tail-pipe level. Another model to scratch from the list. Besides, didn't these people realize that if I could afford one of their strollers, it was a safe bet I had also got enough money for a car?

Just as with cars, there is a lot of status involved in a stroller. As all babies basically look the same, its vehicular attachment of choice is the best way of expressing pedigree.

"Our baby has to have the best" is a trap many a new family falls into, with the safety angle providing the perfect excuse for the extra expense. These people end up with a stroller, albeit magnificent, with more functions than the bridge of the Star Ship Enterprise and a safety certificate from NASA. The trouble is that it weighs 100 pounds and takes up all the room in the car, which often turns out to be a rusty, 20-year-old Ford with no two doors still the same color.

But before you men get too excited, this is nothing more than yet another Machiavellian plot. Although this is an area that actually appealed to the guys, it was strategically placed and had great significance in the whole scheme of things. While it was the only section that was any fun as far as I was concerned, it also had the unfortunate additional issue of being the singlemost expensive area of the shop. It was highly probable that Mom-to-be would allow Dad-to-be to have made the final decision on which stroller to buy. Or more precisely, he would be fooled into thinking that he had made the decision himself. That effectively would mean it was the man that had spent the greatest amount of money. This of course instantly granted his wife total impunity to make a return trip to spend even more to redress the imbalance. It goes under the banner of equality of the sexes and all that.

As far as I could see, the Mothercares of this world had only missed one money-making opportunity. If at the back of the store they had a walk-in vasectomy clinic, the men would be lining around the block, even if it was offered without anesthetic.

Luckily, as that service wouldn't be a requirement for me, I could go home in suitable shape to be ready and able for the rush of passion my wife was likely to have after spending all that money.

LETTER TO DAD

Dad, has it been three months already? Wow! How time flies when you're developing. Sorry about the fish question. Obviously I was just a tad impatient and jumped to the wrong conclusion. My fingers and toes made a successful bid for independence and shed the webbing. They can all wiggle separately and I even have fingerprints now. I guess my days of crime are over.

More great news – I can pee! What a fantastic feeling that is. I just want to do it all the time, which I pretty much can, as I've been storing this stuff up for a while now. It warms the whole place up as well.

Dad, there is one thing I'm quite worried about. My head is HUGE. It must be as big as the rest of my body combined. Is that normal or are we some kind of super-being with a massive brain? I think I look like some sort of cartoon character, which is hardly intellectual. I don't think my little legs would ever be able to hold the rest of me up. So what are they for then? Do we have to lie down the whole time the same as I do in here? I was hoping to be able to stretch out a bit once I got out. Or do we just have to roll around whenever we want to go anywhere?

CHAPTER 9

FITNESS

DURING THE COURSE OF a nine-month-long pregnancy, it stands to reason that even the dumbest amongst us (yes, that means me) is going to come up with a good idea. And as I approached roughly the half-way mark of my journey, I think I finally had one.

As previously described in one of my rare reflective moments, my father had not exactly been "hands-on" while I was growing up. He was what I described a "passive" parent. I decided that I was going to do things differently. By the time my child arrived, I was going to be in suitable condition to be actively involved in everything: I was going to get fit.

For starters, it occurred to me that there was going to be some heavy lifting involved with offspring. My mentally and financially debilitating trip to Mothercare had proved that there was a lot of equipment used in bringing up children: Car seats, strollers, cribs to be assembled, huge bags of supplies to carry around, not to mention the little bundle of joy itself.

I did not consider myself in too bad shape to start with, as I could hold myself up against most of my peers in the office. At least I had not turned "fat and forty." Well, not *that* fat, anyway. But I would have to concede I was some way above my fighting weight and most of my bulges were in the wrong places. Why have a six-pack when you can have the whole barrel, I always used to say when challenged about the size of my stomach. Anyway, round *is* a shape.

With another nod of gratitude to the human gestation period being nine months, I embarked on a fitness campaign.

I only lived about seven miles from the office, so my first drastic step was to say goodbye to the daily taxi ride and dust the cobwebs off my old mountain bike. There were no hills worth worrying about, so a gentle cycle ride to work shouldn't kill me. I must confess that in the early days, particularly after a long session at the bar, I mean office, there were occasions when the bike didn't make it home for the evening. But gradually I improved my stamina, and having started out at a sensible three days a week, I was soon riding in every day. Being a half-hour journey (yes, a mere 14 miles an hour to all the mathematicians out there), without too much effort I had conjured up an hour-a-day fitness routine. For once, I was quite impressed with myself.

I'm fortunate to have a corporate membership to a gym near the office, so having arrived a sweaty mess after cycling, I could take a quick shower, change and go to work. Gradually, my curiosity got the better of me and I decided to see what some of these funky-looking contraptions in the gym were for. Actually, it was more a case of getting fed up with the far-too-young gym staff who saw me leaving a mere 15 minutes after my arrival every day and would always ask "finished already?"

So now, not only was I cycling to work every day, I was also doing some extremely minor weights and even a few stomach exercises when I summoned up enough enthusiasm. It helped if it was raining when I was due to go home, as I would play about in the gym for a while in the hope it would stop before I had to get on the bike. As I was chiseling out this new body, I didn't want it to rust.

Exercise alone though, evidently, was not good enough. I had a more than healthy appetite and that would have to be curtailed to achieve my objective. The good news I received from my personal trainer — a fortieth birthday present from my lovely wife, no subtlety involved — was that it wasn't a case of my eating too much, but rather it was that I had bad eating habits. I ate the wrong things at the wrong times.

I would usually skip breakfast, sometimes even work through lunch and be starving by the time I got home, requiring a huge evening meal that I would then sleep on and turn into fat during my dreams. There was also the danger that when you let yourself get that hungry, you eat whatever is most immediately available, which is inevitably the worst thing: snacks, chips, candy and junk food. Come to think of it, my very portly father used to do exactly the same, so I should have realized a lot sooner where it was going to end up.

My trainer (who thought he had achieved permanent employment by getting me as a client) told me that the long gaps between meals slowed down my metabolism. They made my body store as much food as possible, as it had no idea how long it would be before the next package of energy was going to arrive. If this store of goodies was not used, then it turned into fat. A series of smaller, more regular meals kept the metabolism going faster, burning all the fat as my body knew the next shipment would be along soon. He equated it to putting logs on a fire. If you throw on one huge log, it's overpowering and the fire will take a long time before it eventually takes hold and burns. If you keep putting small logs on at regular intervals, you get a roaring flame.

So, like a little kid going off to school, I started preparing myself a lunch-box to take to work. A couple of sandwiches, some fruit and a few other munchies that weren't too unhealthy and would keep me away from the more dangerous stuff. This also had the added bonus of making my backpack heavier and increasing the benefits of the cycling work-out.

I have to say it was surprisingly easy. After a slow start, the weight began dropping off and in a few months I had lost almost 20 pounds and was looking and feeling a lot better. The improvement was sufficient that even people in the office had noticed and would comment approvingly. This would act as a huge encouragement to keep going, even if making me realize that they obviously all used to think I was a fat slob. I was still easily the weakest guy in the gym in terms of pushing the machines around, but I was making steady progress on getting rid of the bulges of a non-muscle variety.

Should this process continue, there was some hope that I might not put my back out trying to carry the baby into the car seat, or pull a muscle trying to get the stroller out of the trunk. It would mean that when pushing the stroller, I would actually be able to use my arms rather than nudging it along with my belly. Although a long way off in the distant future, I may even be able to participate in school sports day without embarrassing myself, especially as some people would probably think that at my age I must be the kid's grandfather.

It was without doubt one of the best ideas my little brain had come up with since the whole adventure began — or so I thought.

If there can be a bad time to get healthy and lose weight, I had managed to choose the optimum moment. Just as I was shedding the blubber, my lovely wife, being pregnant, was putting on the pounds. It was as if there was a weight transference going on during our sleep and we were heading toward meeting in the middle — and unfortunately I didn't mean of the bed.

Now any guy would consider it eminently logical that a pregnant woman would put on weight. Indeed, only if she were not steadily adding the pounds would it be considered a problem, bearing in mind she was now a party of two. Therefore men would not give it a second thought, or even a first for that matter, which I hadn't. But for women, there is not a single occasion where it is acceptable to be gaining girth. So, while for the first time in years I was actually prepared to risk a pause in front of the mirror, it wasn't long before I faced the inevitable question from my wife, who suspected the mirror would let her down.

"Do I look fat?" she whined.

This is undoubtedly the question that should be the decider on "Who Wants To Be A Millionaire," as it is almost impossible to answer correctly. Obviously "yes," however truthful, is a bad choice and should be avoided at all costs. It would be the most expensive million dollars you had ever won, as you would almost certainly immediately lose half of it along with almost everything else in the divorce settlement.

That leaves "no" as a more viable alternative, but it's not even as simple as that. Which "no" out of the choices B,C, and D should you opt for?

"No" takes on many forms and can have multiple meanings. There is the "silent no," which is the one I apparently use quite often when I tell my wife she can't buy that new dress, or those shoes, or the 10 reference books from Amazon that are all available in the local library. It is conveyed just by a look that isn't suitably approving. Then there's what I call the "impatient no," which is the one my wife uses when I ask for something. The label "impatient" comes from the fact I very rarely get to finish the question before the negative verdict has been given.

"Honey, would it be ok if a few of the guys and I…"

"NO."

"I was going to say take you out for a champagne dinner, but never mind."

"No you weren't. And Billi, Claire and I had a champagne lunch yesterday, so you needn't worry."

Then there's the "instantaneous no," which involves any

request I may have of a sexual nature. This can also take the form of "get off"; "put it away," and its more stringent cousin, "never."

However, in the context of the "fat" question, it's our old favourite the "hesitant no," which is going to land you in the most hot water. Any hint of delay in the answer, any trace of an in-this-case very aptly named "pregnant pause," and your seemingly correct answer of no is totally invalidated. You go immediately to jail, you do not pass go, you certainly do not collect a million dollars.

Still, don't be fooled into thinking that you can borrow the wife's "instantaneous no" to get you out of trouble. Answer too fast and it's like a false start in athletics. The red flag is up and you all have to go back to the beginning and start again.

"You're just saying that. You didn't even think about it, you just said no immediately."

"I don't need to think about it darling, I know you're not fat. You look gorgeous."

The added compliment is an outright gamble. A sort of double-or-quits. If you're lucky, there will be a momentary spot of weakness from the wife and she will buy it, but more likely it's one step too far and she will see through you like a clean pain of glass. Of course "you look gorgeous" is still preferable to the more direct, "well I'd still jump you" approach, which historically has met with very limited success and is more often greeted with a great deal of abuse.

Trying not to answer the question directly and going with a tangential approach is also fraught with danger. The worst offense under these circumstances is the use of logic, which almost always proves catastrophic because you're the only one in the relationship who is still in possession of the said faculty.

So the response "but you're pregnant," isn't going to save your bacon. Quite the opposite to the "silent no," this is what we call the "screaming yes." It's not said out loud, but it's the elephant in the room. The worst thing is you can't even take it back because you never actually said it in the first place, but it's out there in flashing neon lights.

Deafness is not a bad defense. Obviously, you rule out the possibility of answering the question correctly, but looking at the odds, discretion is probably the better part of valor and all that.

"Sorry darling, what was that? Did you say something?"

This can then buy you the necessary time to cut the question off at the pass before it has a chance to rear its ugly head once again. As they say, offense is the best form of defense.

"You're looking nice today," you say. "That color looks good on you."

This may be sufficient to create some confusion and deflect the "fat" question altogether. It takes most of the nine months to learn the trick, but it is possible to use a pregnant woman's absent-mindedness in your favor.

Unfortunately during the course of the pregnancy, this is a question that you're going to have to face many times, with the answer becoming more and more glaringly obvious as each week goes by. Various versions of the question will appear to try to catch you out, such as the conditional alternative.

"Do I look fat in this dress?"

Even though as soon as you look at the dress you're reminded of your last camping trip, there's no need to panic. This is actually pretty easy if you take a legal approach to the question and stick strictly to the actual words used, rather than the intended meaning. In which case the answer is very simple.

"No, not at all darling."

You can say this with conviction and sincerity because it is true as long as we hold on to the phrase "in this dress." Claudia Schiffer would not look fat in that dress; your wife will not resemble Claudia when she takes the dress off, so it's pretty obvious to conclude that the dress is free and clear of all blame here. However, the answer "It's not the dress's fault, love," is the banana skin that's right there to slip up on. Again, the tangential approach could be your savior.

"I always liked that dress" is a good non-committal answer. It's a straightforward statement of fact that can be taken many different ways, with none of them offensive. If you get the feeling your wife is in a particularly negative mood and has already answered the question for herself and is about to change into another outfit, the negative version can be acceptable.

"That dress was never my favourite."

There is only one golden rule in all of this as far as your wife's clothing is concerned, and it comes in two parts.

The first part is the set up: It doesn't really concern the man at all and there's little that can be done to avoid it. The fact is that as soon as your wife puts on a few pounds and can't fit into the smallest, tightest, sexiest outfit that she possesses, she is going to take the credit card down to the maternity shop and splurge on a whole new range of designer garments, most of which are destined never to be worn.

As an aside, and going back to the "fat" question, I strenuously suggest that any other Pregnant Guys out there loiter at a maternity shop one afternoon for the purposes of education.

The women who work in these shops are qualified experts at complimenting pregnant women. They must know exactly the right thing to say on every occasion, because somehow they talk them into spending an absolute fortune buying A-frame tents that pass as dresses and jeans that the fattest construction worker would easily get into. They can also seem to get away with suggesting something doesn't quite look right without making it sound as if your wife looks like a hippo. These people should run courses.

Anyway, your wife has bought all these maternity clothes. So what's the golden rule? Basically, it's as easy as this.

Avoid logic at all times. We all know the reason she went down to the maternity shop in the first place was because she was too big to get into her normal clothes. The word "maternity" is a major clue as to why she needs bigger clothes, but none of this matters.

At no point must you *ever* suggest your wife wear her maternity clothes. Voicing this opinion goes way beyond the "screaming yes" mistake and takes you to a whole new level of suffering. She will attempt to suck you into it by trying to wear all her normal clothes and complaining they don't fit, leaving you to make the obvious suggestion of wearing the maternity dress. After all, being pregnant, isn't that why she bought it? Again, remember the man is the only one possessing logic. It's a barren planet as far as pregnant women are concerned.

Nothing shouts "you're fat" like telling someone to wear maternity clothes. As I'm writing this book, you may correctly conclude that this was luckily one of the few mistakes I did not make, otherwise I probably would have had a third and unplanned opening of my scrotal sack to contend with.

It's from these expert sales women that I actually picked up our old favorite "radiant." It can cover a multitude of situations, can mean almost anything you want it to mean and is quite obviously complimentary.

So, where were we? Ah yes. I was getting fit and shedding the pounds like a boxer before a prize fight; my wife was piling them on and getting fatter than a pig heading to market. It was like a train wreck waiting to happen. One heading north, the other south, and there's only one track. We could all see the accident coming, but no one could do anything to stop it.

When it got to the stage my wife couldn't fit into her jeans any more, the thought that she could instead wear mine, which were by then too big for me, was only a split-second away from becoming an audible suggestion and a colossal error of judgment.

I decided the best course of action was to take my fitness

regime to the next level to try to avoid the inevitable. I had to start doing some weight-training and hope that I could put some muscle on my feeble frame. After all, they say muscle weighs more than fat, so I might be able to gain a few pounds and ensure the dreaded crossover never occurred.

I didn't like doing weights at all. It was hard work, and more to the point it was embarrassing that I had to reduce the weight-stack from the woman who was using the apparatus before me. I thought the bar alone was quite heavy, before you started loading anything onto it. My physique owed more to the type of bar you sit at rather than lift. I even thought about wearing some kind of sports bandage on my knee or elbow, so I could at least make it look like I was recovering from an injury, rather than just being weak and pathetic.

It was all very well for these movie stars who worked out for three hours a day, six days a week. First of all, they had a dedicated personal trainer, whereas mine had been just a loaner. Secondly, they didn't have a day job to go to for 10 hours first. I was sure that if fitness was the only work I did for a couple of months, even I could look a bit buff, or cut, or whatever the relevant gym-speak is for not looking like a blob.

I had also discovered that working out in the gym was very bad for my other faculties. My ability to do math was one of the first things that went. Once I started getting tired, which occurred pretty shortly after I began, I found I couldn't count any more. Sets of 10 become 5,6,7, – 10. Then my ability to tell the time started to erode as my 20 minutes on the treadmill was all done inside 12.

Despite having set my sights suitably low, I was comfortably able to fall short. Luckily, I had worked on the basis that anything I did in the gym, however pitiful, was still better than not doing it and on that basis could still be considered a success.

In an effort to give myself a goal to aim for, I even signed up for a charity run of a mere 4 miles or so. A bunch of people from the office were doing it, so once I had signed on the dotted line, there was no backing out. This would give me the incentive to put in the extra training and take me to the next level.

If you ever wondered what inspired Henry Ford to invent the car, my guess is that he entered a charity run and realized how far four miles was and that there had to be a better way.

Now walking four miles or more when playing a round of golf is a different matter. All of us guys, in whatever state of disrepair we find ourselves, can manage to drag a set of clubs around a course for a few hours. The trick is there's a purpose to it. This was running just for the sake of running. It wasn't even like I was going anywhere, as a circular course brought me right back to where I started — what was the point of that? Why couldn't I at least start four miles from my house and run home? Wouldn't that make infinitely more sense?

For training purposes, that's exactly what I did. I mapped out a two-mile stretch from my door with the intention of running there and back after work. Not being an idiot, the first time I went I made sure I had cab money with me in case I faded. I'm proud to say that I didn't need to use it, although whether there was more running or walking involved in the journey, I'm not sure. However each time I tried it, the running became more and the walking less.

When the fateful day came, all I can say is that I achieved my extremely lowly ambition of completing the entire course without being reduced to walking at any point. My more lofty goal of finishing within half an hour was quite easily unchallenged as older, fatter colleagues left me in their dust. I am certainly wiser for the experience though, and the one valuable lesson I learned from doing a four-mile run is that I never intend to run five. From now on, I wouldn't even run for a bus.

Still, I grew in fitness little by little; the weight came off pound by pound; the belt started to have a purpose, rather than just being a fashion item; and the reflection in the mirror started to resemble someone I knew many years ago.

So as I grew confident that I looked the best I had done for ages, I reassured myself with the knowledge that when we reached the part of the pregnancy when my wife turned into a raving nymphomaniac, I would be more than capable of the demands made of me.

LETTER TO DAD

Hi Dad. You were right about my head. It took a couple of months but all my proportions are starting to look a lot more sensible now. I'm not so worried about falling over all the time. How come you know all this stuff? Do you still have a massive head?

However, you could have warned me about the headaches. The people upstairs are still having work done and now that I have ears it's a lot louder. They must be behind schedule because there's constant bashing going on. It never stops, 24-7, even at the weekends. I think they might be doing the bathrooms at the moment, judging by all the gurgling noises I keep hearing. (Mind you, who can blame them when peeing is so much fun. I'm still loving doing that.)

Or maybe they're getting some windows put in. I know I'd sure like to have a window now that my eyes are working. A womb with a view — that would be sweet.

There's not a great deal to do here so I've been practicing my breathing for when I get out. Is it out-in or in-out? I can never seem to remember where to start. Which one is more important? I'll practice that one first and worry about the other one later. It shouldn't take me too long to get the hang of it.

Dad, if it's ok, the first thing I want to do when I get home is go for something decent to eat. The food here is awful. Same old crap day in and day out. Oh look, amniotic fluid again. I can't understand why I've been given taste buds when I don't ever get anything different to try. Honestly, prisoners get treated better than this. Even the guys on death row get to choose their own meal. Dad, are you punishing me for something? Is that why I'm being kept in the dark and in solitary confinement?

Can we go for a hamburger or a juicy steak? Please tell me we're not vegetarians, or vegans or something. I'm not going to be born into some commune and live off lentils and brown rice am I?

CHAPTER 10

VILLAGE IDIOT

THERE'S ONE POINT I would like to mention before we get into the home stretch and the actual birth. This may go some way to explaining why I had a decent amount of trepidation as I embarked on my "Journey to the Center of the Birth."

My darling wife is a Childbirth Educator. Now that may well sound scary, but let me tell you, scary isn't even the half of it. She owns and runs a company that, among other things, offers classes that start out with prenatal schooling for parents-to-be and goes right through pregnancy, labor, birth and even includes breast-feeding classes once the baby is born. She is also qualified and practices as what's known as a "doula," which is a person who supports a woman through labor and childbirth.

Probably the simplest way to describe her role is that she has a similar function to that of a midwife, with the notable exception that she does not undertake any form of medical procedure. For the lucky mother, it's almost like having a personal coach to help her through the big event. And seeing as the training required to have a baby is an enforced nine-month course, it doesn't sound like a bad idea at all. Another description of what a doula does is "Mothering the Mother."

The motto of her company is "Your Birth, Your Way," which really sums up her approach to childbirth. The aim is not to tell a woman how her birth should be, to steer someone down what she considers to be a pre-determined path to what she would prefer to define as the best birth. But rather she aims to provide an expectant mother with as much information as possible, so that the mother can make informed choices about what she wants to happen to her body during the birth of her child.

I'm relieved to say my wife is far from being a hairy-arm-pitted, organic-lentil eating tree-hugger on some crusade to make women have natural births without doctors or hospitals in sight. If that's what a woman wants, all well and good, she can certainly have it. If, however, she prefers to take every drug known to man, perhaps a few new experimental ones on top of that, and have more medical back-up than an episode of ER, then that's equally fine too.

The role of the doula is one of support and encouragement, to help ensure that once a woman has chosen the type of birth she wants, she gets the type of birth she chose. Often a woman starts her pregnancy declaring her birth will be "all natural, drug free, I-Am-Woman-Hear-Me-Roar," but actually ends up being "Hook me up to that f-ing epidural now and get this thing out — wake me when it's over." The important aspect is that by the time she gets to give birth, she knows what she wants and she understands what she needs to do to achieve it.

I think it's a wonderful job, or perhaps I should call it a vocation, and she is fabulous at it. Of course I take a great deal of pride in this, as after years of putting up with me, even the most difficult client is a comparative breeze.

Also, I have now watched firsthand how my own wife's thought process has slowly and steadily disintegrated during her own pregnancy, to the state where simply making a cup of tea can sometimes be an ordeal that reduces her to tears. On that basis alone, the chances of making the correct decision during the throes of labor, or remembering anything other than "this hurts," would seem unlikely. So to have a trained expert there at a mother's side to remind her of the wishes she had expressed and to support her belief that it's the right thing to do as the doubts start creeping in must be a Godsend.

For once in pregnancy, a doula also is something that is actually of great benefit to the father, amazing as that may sound. The mere presence of a doula at a birth removes men from having to make any decisions. Everything should follow a pre-arranged birth-plan, in which the mother outlines her preferences concerning certain eventualities, which were made when she was in a sounder state of mind. The doula is there to remind, help and encourage her to follow through on those decisions.

As a result, the man doesn't have to make a bad call under pressure, which would doubtless be thrown back in his face for retribution at some, or probably many, later dates. Our child's failure to make college could well be scientifically traced back to my impaired judgment in allowing someone to change the

CD during the birth process.

I know many new fathers who now hold my wife in the highest regard, because she acted as a bodyguard, selflessly stepping in front of his wife's bullets and sparing him the wounds. She also has the ability to ensure the father is supportive at the right times and standing well back at the right times, improving everyone's experience.

So what makes her job such a problem, I hear you ask?

Well, as you now know I was dragged somewhat reluctantly into the entire baby-making affair to start with, it's probably not going to take a big stretch of your imagination to work out I'm not exactly an expert on the subject. I have studiously avoided all things to do with babies my entire life — and with great success, I may add. When friends have children, I simply cross them off the Christmas-card list and move on. I have no intention of ever going to their house again and risk being confronted with the little bugger. I don't even want to see the family photos.

I will confess to being a Godparent, but that's only because the child involved lives in another country and I don't actually see him very often. I'm the mystical foreign guy who keeps sending presents from afar. It's actually an extremely effective relationship. He thinks I'm OK, as the presents are the only thing that really matter. I always dutifully fulfill my role by remembering birthdays and Christmas, which puts me well ahead even of some of his own relatives. The fact that I live abroad also means my presents are somewhat different from the usual fare, giving me extra street cred.

I only took on the job because I knew how much my friend's own Godfather had meant to him, and therefore what a stupendous honor it was to have been asked to take on that role for his first-born son. So I would never have been so churlish as to refuse the request just because of the minor technicality of not actually liking children. Besides, the trio of Marlon Brando, Robert de Niro and Al Pacino had all made the job designation distinctly cool.

And when I say that I didn't like children, I really did mean it. There was no "very much" or "yet" attached to the statement. I didn't like a lot of them when I was one myself, nor they me to be fair, and the feeling hadn't mellowed with age. A woman can't walk past a baby without smiling and saying how cute it looks. I can't walk past a baby without looking the other way.

First of all, they all look almost exactly the same — Oh yes they do. Perhaps to the actual parents, their own babies look different, and no doubt better than the average infant. I mean I guess that makes sense, or it would get confusing and they would all take the wrong one home from playgroup. But come on, apart from the clothing, they are all practically identical — pudgy little Michelin boys and girls that appear to have had way too many collagen injections. And they are all very noisy — incredibly so for their tiny size, with amazing stamina when it comes to screaming the place down for no apparent reason. Why is it that a baby's lungs develop about a decade in advance of everything else on its little body? A group of babies reminds me of a little nest of newborn birds, all looking the same and squawking the same.

So, it should be no surprise that when it comes to having babies, I'm the village idiot compared with my wife, who is a veritable fountain of knowledge. As a doula, she offers people practical information on every aspect of pregnancy, which of course means she has to know about every possible variable of pregnancy, in very minute detail.

I don't even score good marks on the practical side of it, despite repeated requests to my wife to be allowed to do more training. According to her, rather than a Childbirth educator, I am in much greater need of a Child "Making" educator.

Normally, this would be a situation she would absolutely relish — the opportunity to laud her intellectual superiority over me on a regular basis and in public. Except that now it had become personal, I could only imagine that my ignorance of all things baby-related must have scared her almost as much as it did me. Her campaign to coerce me into having a child had been very much steeped in the theoretical, the *idea* of us having a baby. I had to guess she had never stopped to think of the aftermath of that decision, when we were left with a living, breathing entity that needed to be constantly cared for — and I was talking about me.

Rather than helpful support, I was more likely to be a total hindrance, requiring more adult supervision than the baby. For starters, part of the contract I had drawn up stated quite categorically that the changing of dirty diapers was not on the agenda as far as I was concerned. As my wife would be breast-feeding our little bundle of joy, it seemed more than fair to me that as she was the person who put it in one end, she could deal with it when it came back out of the other.

Besides, on the few occasions I had ever tried to do anything around the house I had shown an amazing lack of manual dexterity. Plumbers, painters, carpenters and the like made a good living off people like me. I would make such a compete botch-up of whatever task I attempted, it would result in the experts having to be called in and winning a job that would cost at least twice as much than if I had simply hired them to do it in the first place.

I was sure it would be the same with a baby. The poor little thing would probably end up with both legs in one side of the diaper and an arm through the other hole, leaving it completely unprotected and able to pee all over the floor when the need arose. I know I have stated that I didn't like children, but I didn't believe in being needlessly cruel to them either.

The other big issue with my idiocy cropped up whenever we were out with friends. If a man was a pilot, no one would expect his wife to know how to fly a plane, and rightly so. Yet for me, because my wife was a doula, for some inexplicable reason, I was also meant to be a walking dictionary on all things to do with birth.

Instead, I was a complete embarrassment with a blank, ignorant expression usually being the best I could offer. That still was always preferable to my attempting to actually answer a question and making a total fool of myself. Best to be thought an idiot, than to open your mouth and prove it, I believe the proverb goes.

If there had to be a test before you could have children, I would surely fail. (And let's be honest here, it's not a bad idea. The government should seriously consider it. In England you need a license just to get a television.) Evolution has got to a stage of development where we really don't need any more people like me. Perhaps nature would have its own way of redressing the balance, as I seriously doubted any child left in my care would last more than a few days at most.

Actually, it gets even worse than that. Just as some of my friends are also journalists, it stands to reason that some of my wife's friends are also in the childbirth business. So basically, they're all experts on breeding and they all talk about babies more often than guys talk about sports. You may not think that's possible, but welcome to the hell that I live in.

An exaggeration? Not even close. When I say they talk about babies, I don't even mean they tell sweet stories about what little Johnny did, or how much someone's baby looks like its mother, father, sister or brother. Or the much more exciting, how much little Johnny *doesn't* look like his brother, sister or father, who was on a business trip roughly nine months ago.

What I mean is, they talk about birth as in the physical act of: All the gory details; the blow-by-blow, or rather push-by-push, account of how another little soul came into the world. In glorious Technicolor, unedited, uncensored and X-Rated. If Quentin Tarantino did a movie about birth, these women would be his technical consultants for all the blood and guts.

The only saving grace is they use a lot of technical, Latin-sounding words that I don't understand, which spared me from some of the more horrific descriptions of bodily functions and fluids. They say that once someone has worked in the Mars factory, that person will never want to eat a chocolate bar again — so, how much do you imagine I wanted a child?

Oh, by the way. My wife had kindly invited every single one of the other doulas she worked with to attend her birth. Yes, that's right. I was going to have to become a father under the glare of half a dozen experts who would all be watching my every move, taking notes on my every mistake. I would be the ham at the Jewish wedding.

The one thing I will say in my wife's defense is that she was smart enough to realize she was not the one who should be in charge of my education in impending fatherhood. If she was ever to write a book, I know she would absolutely detest the idea of me peering over her shoulder giving advice and suggestions, or even worse, uttering small tut-tutting sounds and shaking my head in disapproval of some minor error in syntax.

As guys, we can all remember when we tried to teach our teenage girlfriends how to drive. (By this I mean we were also teenagers, not that we were in our thirties and still dating teenagers.) Anyway, the usual result was that we needed a new gearbox, front-wing, rear bumper and probably a new girlfriend.

Adults in general do not like being told what to do, even

when they quite patently don't know how to do whatever it is that they are trying to do. And the closer the relationship of the person doing the telling, the more annoying it is to the person being told. Most of us would rather accept assistance from a complete stranger before admitting to our partner we were totally incompetent, completely at a loss and needed their help.

What I did notice was that a few books strategically started to be left lying around in tactical spots where I was bound to see them. Or a magazine would be left open at the appropriate page where an article on fatherhood could be found. DVD offerings of Robin Williams or Billy Connolly talking about parenthood would appear, to try to nudge me toward the impression that babies can indeed be a lot of fun and make you laugh.

Surprisingly, as I started to read a few of the shorter offerings, I realized that some of the incessant chatter I had been exposed to had filtered through the haze and I actually knew one or two things. The other reassurance was that while I may well hold the title of Village Idiot, it was a fiercely fought contest among the male species and I was not bringing down the average IQ of "Man Village" by more than a few points.

Women are born with maternal instincts — it could even be said that their ultimate achievement on earth is to create another life. They happen to be extremely good at it and they don't need any help. No surprise then, that we men have absolutely no trace of paternal leanings whatsoever until after the little bundle arrives, when a form of survival training kicks in, both for the father and the baby.

For men, it was very much a learn-as-you-go process, and we just hoped to stay one step, you could even say one baby step, ahead of the child. When you hear of friends having problems with their children, it has always been my view that was because the child has read a couple of chapters of the manual ahead of schedule and has pulled out a slight lead, leaving the parents struggling to catch up.

My reluctance at least ensured that I didn't fall into the trap of many an impending father and become too involved in my wife's pregnancy. Now, I'm not implying that husbands should appear disinterested in their wife's condition, as that would have catastrophic consequences, very much like being in the lion's den and not watching the lion. However, there was no getting away from the truth that it was indeed your wife that was pregnant and it was your wife that would be having the baby.

When my wife decides that I need to be more involved at any particular juncture in the proceedings, she has a very clear, often violent, way of getting that message across to me. Equally, when she deems she is in need of a bit more space, the "back off" signal is brighter than a Naval flare on a dark night.

Some men make the mistake of trying to be so wrapped up in the whole process that they start to think they are actually the one that is pregnant. They are genuinely disappointed that they can't spread their legs akimbo and squeeze out the baby themselves. They turn into "Adam," the first man on earth to ever have a child. They are the procreational equivalent of Born-Again Christians. They have seen the light and now they need to preach to the world until everyone else sees the same light as them.

Although if ever there was a lesson in the perils of being careful about what you wish for, Adam is certainly it. I seem to recall all he got out of the deal was an apple and an eviction order from the Garden of Eden. And probably an alimony bill from Eve.

We men have to learn very quickly how difficult, not to mention dangerous, it is to live with an overly hormonal woman who is susceptible to the most illogical acts at the most inauspicious times. So imagine how utterly unbearable it must be for the said hormonal woman to cope with an equally hormonal man. "Sharing" is not the same as "supporting," so when your wife is eight months pregnant and complaining of swollen feet and chronic back pain, the response, "I know honey, me too. Could you get me a beer from the fridge," isn't likely to go down very well. For once, being an unfeeling, unemotional, unsympathetic man was actually going to work in my favor. Or at least not work against me as much as usual.

Anyway, I was going to need to save all of my unbridled love and support for when my wife would reach a stage of her pregnancy that turned her into a raving nymphomaniac. She was going to need my help then and I was ready to be overly generous. I had even been working on a new apology.

LETTER TO DAD

Dad, I noticed a couple of weeks ago I'd started growing this fine hair all over my body. (It's called lanugo, probably after some Italian.) At first I thought I might have been a monkey, but then I realized I didn't have a tail and wasn't craving bananas, so it seemed unlikely. I know, I know, the whole fish scare all over again, sorry. I never learn do I? Anyway, my point is I don't want to end up being mothered by someone who has a ton of it under her armpits.

Dad, are you going to be a good Dad? Have you been to some sort of training school to learn what to do? Did you get lessons from your own father? What exactly do Dads have to do anyway? I'm going to do my best to be a really good baby for you. I've had loads of sleep since I've been in here, so I'll barely need any rest at all when I get out. So we can stay up all night and play. Won't that be fun? I know this really cool game where I cry and you have to guess what I want. It's really great and I can play for hours and hours. Otherwise, I'm always happy to pee on you — you don't even have to ask.

Dad, the landlord has given me a month to leave. He's not very friendly at all. He reminded me that if I overstay my welcome, he knows this mean-looking guy in a mask who will come and drag me out by force if necessary. Frankly, I'll be glad to see the back of this place as I am definitely growing out of it. There's barely room to swing a cat in here and I can't remember the last time I was really able to stretch my legs.

CHAPTER 11

BACK TO SCHOOL

PRE-NATAL CLASSES. SO WHAT was all that about? The opening salvo of conversation, or more precisely negotiation, between my wife and me did not get off to a good start. I opted for that old sports technique of attack being the best form of defense. All I can say is whoever came up with that idea was most definitely a single man. Attack, so it proved, was the best form of getting annihilated even quicker than when you played defensively.

I began by asking why I needed to go. After all, it wasn't me that was going to have this baby. What did I need to learn? How to watch? I already knew how to open a bottle of champagne, how to circumcise a cigar and torch it in a plume of smoke. Those were the two traditional duties a father-to-be was required to perform. Surely this class wasn't necessary for me?

I got a two-word answer. Well yes, those more infamous two words were involved as well, but technically they didn't actually qualify as an answer, more of an instruction. The two words to which I refer in this context were "Moral Support." I needed to be there because she needed me to be there. This was a tricky one to deal with. It was, after all, one of those rare times my wife actually had confessed that she needed me for anything at all. She had also managed to use the word "need" in the correct sense, as opposed to the more familiar context of "I need another pair of shoes."

My wife the doula, the Childbirth expert, had said that she *needed* me. It was a cunning ploy to stroke my ego and lull me into believing that I may even have a role to play in this most female of exploits. My wife was letting me think that she could not do this without me. Just as certainly as I knew this to be a bald-faced lie, so too did I know that I would be attending pre-natal classes.

Through the thin veil of deception I realized the task being asked of me was actually one I could perform with admirable ease. When you cut to the chase, my presence was being requested so that I could look, and most likely be, stupid, so that my wife didn't. The only skill I required was the fine line of not being so stupid that I became a cause of embarrassment to my wife, who would then have to start apologizing for me. Hopefully, some other unwitting husband or partner would fill that role and I could get away with appearing only mildly retarded.

One thing I naively did fail to immediately notice was the use of the plural in the word "classes." How hard was this childbirth business meant to be? Did you have to get a degree in it before you were allowed to bring an extra little being into the world? Was the reason the human gestation period was nine months long because there was apparently an inordinate amount that had to be studied and researched before you were anywhere close to being ready to be a parent? Or was it simply that because pregnancy lasted for the best part of a year, there was an awful lot of spare time to kill?

Still, as about the only thing I knew for sure about birth and parenting was that I knew absolutely nothing at all about birth and parenting, I conceded that my presence probably wouldn't be a bad idea. They say you learn something new every day, so attending these classes would at least provide me with a few days where I made my quota.

The other positive factor (and I was scratching around trying to find some), was that I could say I was being included in something. Although I had been living vicariously as the Pregnant Guy, there was actually precious little to do during the entire proceedings. It could be quite easy to feel left out and very much surplus to requirements. Even though as her husband, my wife had often turned to me for advice or simply to be her sounding board, pregnancy was the notable exception. Women needed to talk to other women about this kind of stuff. And if I was being honest, I was more than ok with that.

I would just have to content myself with the fact I could add one more item to the very short list of achievements when I had actually been "needed." Now the tasks of opening a jar and dealing with a wasp had a new companion.

When the first day of school dawned, I was dragged reluctantly from the house like the proverbial dog being taken to the kennels. My facial expression was akin to someone who had just licked a stinging nettle. The warm glow of being needed had long since been replaced by utter reluctance and the knowledge I was going to embarrass both myself and my wife — repeatedly.

Pre-natal classes are, as you would expect, organized and run entirely by women. That included the scheduling, which was why they always seemed to fall on evenings when there was an important sporting event to be watched. My wife had a good point in commenting that I had previously never shown much interest in following badminton, but even had it been the Super Bowl, I still would have had no choice but to hit the kill switch and sulk my way out the front door. I felt like the kid going to school knowing he hasn't done his homework and that detention was a foregone conclusion. Nothing good could come from this.

My mood was not enhanced upon arrival at a sterile, school-type place with all the warmth and charm of a prison visiting room. Whatever we had paid for the classes, the proceeds were obviously not invested in the decorations. Nor had they blown the budget on the chairs. They must have searched many furniture stores to find something as uncomfortable as these seats. Of course all the pregnant Moms had generated some extra padding in the past few months, so they didn't seem to notice. But a few of the Dads appeared distinctly ill at ease. Mind you, if they were anything like me, they didn't need the chairs for that.

I was not sure what else this room had been used for other

than interrogation, but I didn't find it as difficult as I had expected to pay attention to the proceedings, as the surroundings were totally devoid of any other distractions. No carpets on the floor, no pictures on the walls, save for a few shaded areas where they had once hung. Maybe that was a blessing. A couple of poster-sized photos of Mothers in the throes of childbirth, or newborn babes before they had been cleaned and polished, could well have been enough to send the men running for the door, screaming.

The guys all eyed each other sympathetically. We were all somewhat relieved that at least we were not alone in this endeavor of probable humiliation. We were not the only men to be totally governed by our other halves. Having said that, in my experience men can be divided into two categories. Those that were subservient to their wives, were aware of it, and had learned to be at peace with the situation. Alternatively, there were the men who were still walking tall and proud and were in charge of everything. What they say, went, and all that. This second group of men was also controlled by their wives. The only difference was, sadly, they simply hadn't cottoned on to the fact yet.

I don't know if the other men did this — and if they admitted to it I'm sure they would come up with a similar answer — but being a totally shallow and pathetic man, the first thing I did was to scope out the other wives for some instant comparisons. I was pleased to discover that my wife was without question going to be the "Yummy-Mummy" of the group. She also seemed to be enduring her pregnancy with some style, compared with a few others. This helped to keep our class average up as a couple and went some way to compensate for the fact that I had also spotted I was easily the oldest Daddy in the group. Some of the guys here looked like they had only just finished being kids, rather than being old enough to have them. Any of the Moms surveying the gathering to see how their man shaped up would also have looked at him more favorably after seeing me. How often do we see or meet other couples and the first thing that flashes through our mind is "what on earth is she/he doing with him/her?" Love is indeed blind, or blind drunk at a minimum.

In yet another sign that this event was totally organized by women, I immediately noted there was no bar anywhere in sight. Nothing on offer stronger than a kettle and a few tea bags that looked like they had been recycled a couple of times. Now I knew that women weren't supposed to drink during pregnancy, but I had not read about any such restrictions for the guys. You would have thought at a gathering like this, where much courage was needed by all men just to turn up, a little bit of the Dutch variety in the form of alcohol could have been on offer as a welcoming gesture. I always wonder what the Dutch did to become renowned for being somewhat less than heroic? Still, if drinks had to be ordered, at least you knew they would pay half of the bill.

Now I was not saying that I needed a cocktail waiter, but a fridge full of beer would certainly have taken the edge off the mens' nerves and put us all more at ease. After all, weren't we guys meant to be getting in touch with our emotions and opening up? (The phrase reminded me of surgery and caused an instinctive twinge in my battle-scarred scrotum.) Wouldn't a couple of cold ones at least have made everyone a little more chatty?

With just enough time to wring some flavor out of one of the second-hand tea bags (which I feared was herbal as well. Was there no respite?) me and my chipped cup were asked to take our places so the fun could begin. We were spread out in a non-confrontational circle, so we all sat there like guilty children, avoiding looking at each other and waiting for someone else to do or say something. As I was staring at the floor to see whether I could spot the shaded area where a rug used to be, I was quite startled when the woman sitting on my left (who was not my wife) piped up and started talking.

Evidently I had gone and sat right next to the class orchestrator, making me instantly worried the other guys would write me off as a teacher's pet. The only advantage was that I was about the only person that she couldn't make direct eye contact with, which meant I was less likely to get asked a question. She also wouldn't be able to see when I was not paying attention.

True to form at these types of events, she had begun by asking everyone to say who they were and a little bit about themselves. Luckily, she went in a clockwise direction. So as I was at 11 o'clock, I would have some time to work out who I was and what I planned to say.

The others fired off name, rank and serial number in an overly cheery and forced manner, everyone on their best behavior and keen to impress.

It appeared we were in the company of some very intelligent people, judging by the array of job descriptions being thrown around: We had the mandatory computer/IT expert, so I was extremely unlikely to understand a word he said; the prodigal investment banker, who probably earned more than the rest of us put together; one of the Moms was a lawyer; we seemed to have a United Nations cross-section of nationalities as well, starting with us, with me being English and my wife Australian. We also had a New Zealander and a Brazilian man who were married to Chinese women, an American couple, an English woman who was with a very tall, Yao Ming-like fellow and a few people I was actually going to have to talk to further in order to ascertain their exact lineage. What a small world we live in. One woman was here on her own, apologizing for her husband's absence. I was impressed and somewhat envious of her partner's ability to worm his way out of attending. Well done, Sir.

From the group, I was most worried about another English guy who said he was a kindergarten teacher. Evidently, we had a ringer in our midst. I was surrounded by a bunch of people who all seemed to be more intelligent than me and one of whom was a genuine kiddie expert. As I suspected right from the start, and alluded to earlier, I was indeed the village idiot.

Even worse, while this wave of nausea was rushing over me, my time had unknowingly run out and all the academic, expert people were now looking at me and waiting for my presentation.

"Hello, my name is Simon and I've been an alcoholic for three years."

My wife smacked me on the arm, almost covering up a couple of audible gasps from the women at three and eight O'clock.

"I'm so sorry, that's my other group," I said in apology. "Actually, I'm a journalist and I'm planning to write a book about all of this baby stuff. So anyone of you could end up in print if you're not careful."

That shut them up. Suddenly they realized they may indeed be under scrutiny. And as you'll discover if you bother to read any more of this chapter, a few of them will wish they had stayed quiet, as there's nothing you can make up that's funnier than the things people say and do in real life.

So, introductions completed and mostly forgotten, we were off and running. First topic on the agenda, suitably enough, was "Labor Support." I took a wild guess that this could actually apply to me. Wasn't that why I had been brought along? As my wife would obviously be busy with the "labor" portion of the proceedings, that must leave me to handle the "support" end of the bargain. As I feared, rather than giving the abridged version and just telling the men what we needed to do to be supportive, we were going to plod through the entire process of labor from start to finish, contraction by contraction.

Did I need to know how the engine worked to drive the

car? Did I need to kill the bull to eat the beef? Wasn't this all a tad unnecessary? Naturally, these were all rhetorical and very much silent questions. I had not been quite so stupid, for once, as to have aired my misgivings. As the old saying goes, if you're talking, the chances are you're not learning. And there was still so much I needed to learn.

It seemed our journey was going to start at "Early Labor." It sounded like a phase in an artist's life. "Van Gogh painted this in his early labor period." Perhaps the next stages of childbirth would be "Impressionist" and "Renaissance?"

Oh dear. We had barely got going and already my mind had wandered like a drunk stumbling his way home on a Friday night. This could not be a good sign. From what little I did pick up, it seemed early labor was a sort of warm up routine. It was the pre-show performance before the headline star made an appearance. Just some light exercise to get the body toned up and ready for the big event.

Apparently many women, and no doubt even more men, mistake this for the real thing and rush straight to the hospital. Once there, they are laughed at behind their backs by the nursing staff, who must have seen this hundreds of times before, but never fail to find it funny. It was roughly equal to guys thinking they had scored after the girl they had just walked up to in a bar, said "hello." And she was probably the one serving the drinks.

Our teacher informed us that any women who found this early labor painful were in for quite a shock. Apparently on a scale of one to 10, though many women would class this pain as a four or even a five, this was in fact only a one. I wondered at this point whether it was our teacher's first class, as she hadn't exactly put anyone at ease with her rude awakenings. Maybe she was battle-hardened by doing too many classes? Or perhaps she didn't care. After all, it was not as if any of us present could change our minds about having a baby.

Quite what "supportive" comments the husband was supposed to come out with at this juncture I still did not know. Not surprisingly, our oracle of a teacher wasn't providing any suggestions either. At least none of us were put on the spot by being asked for possible solutions.

"Don't even worry about this, honey. Remember, it's going to hurt a heck of a lot more later," was one comment that immediately sprang to my mind. Or perhaps "stop being such a girl, the teacher said this part barely hurts at all."

Well why not? That was the style of supportive comments our sports coaches used to make to us guys, and a lot worse. Come the time, however, I would no doubt wimp out with something inspiring like, "you're doing great, love."

Perhaps past experience had taught the teacher that at this nascent stage of the class, the chance of one of the men being able to give a sensible answer to almost any question was slightly less than zero. She therefore simply didn't bother to ask us and pitched her teaching squarely at the more attentive and responsive, albeit worried, women.

Apparently this early labor act can drag on for days rather than hours and just has to be endured with as good a grace as possible — very akin to my feelings on this class so far. But when the main event arrives, we were told it would mark its entrance in superb style with the breaking of the waters.

It all sounds very biblical and momentous, which I can only imagine couldn't be further from the truth. For this is when the sack of amniotic fluid in which the baby has been encased makes a dash for freedom. I could only guess it felt something similar to not going to the toilet for a week and then wetting yourself. What an absolute joy for my wife to look forward to. She hadn't even had the baby yet, but she was going to start demonstrating the bladder control of one.

The teacher then continued to dissect this phenomenon into the myriad different types of "break" a woman might have. These ranged from a mere trickle right through to a positive Niagara-Falls-like experience, which was really all far too much information for me. By the looks of a few other expressions around our circle, it was even a bit too much for some of the women. My mind started to drift off to drier places.

Suddenly a voice seeped into my consciousness that alerted me to the fact that something significant had changed. For the first time, it was a man's voice. One of the Dads had plucked up the courage to ask a question. Good for you Squire. Step forward and be the first to look stupid. Take one for the team.

Most of us were under the impression that simply being there was showing sufficient support to warrant a medal. But to his dubious credit, he was giving it the old college try. This may even be worth paying attention to, I thought. Hopefully he would ask something really stupid, like, "well if her water is broken, how do we fix it?"

What actually transpired was that he was not so much asking a question as making a statement. Or even worse, challenging what the teacher had said. Is that even allowed in the class rules? I had no idea what he actually said, or whether it made any sense. All I can remember is that it seemed to take forever.

Oh My God! My worst nightmare had been realized. We had got a know-it-all in the class. We had ended up with some guy who had gone and read every single book available. He had immersed himself in an empathic pregnancy with his wife and probably would wet himself at the opportune time so as to fully share the breaking-water experience. There was usually one in every group, but I hadn't been able to pick him out during the introductory merry-go-round. Well, he had certainly revealed his true colors now.

I thought he had quite an impressive beer gut when I met him, but I now feared it was his phantom pregnancy belly, which he had grown in sympathy. As if these sessions weren't going to be long enough, now we had an attention-seeker. We had been lumbered with some guy who was going to prolong proceedings with endless displays of his own gargantuan knowledge of the subject. He would probably end up running the class, given half a chance. I could see similarly pained expressions on the faces of the other know-nothing Dads like me. There was also the worry that if he was going to make continual comments, the rest of us were going to be expected to offer some sort of contribution. He had ruined it for any of us that were looking to fly under the radar.

By contrast, a couple of the women were giving appreciative nods. They would then look askance at their husbands with a withering expression that said "why couldn't you have said something intelligent like that?" Yeah, well the novelty value would soon wear off, and then they would realize, just as I already had, that this guy was going to prove to be a monumental pain in the butt.

It turned out he was training to be some sort of holistic doctor, whatever the heck that was. Perhaps it meant you could get him to diagnose you via the computer? I would have to ask our techy guy at work later. That, or it was something vaguely religious. Either way, I made a mental note that he was to be treated with the utmost suspicion from now on.

It occurred to me that the chances of his wife having a pain-free birth with him chirping away in her ear all the time were slim to none. He wouldn't be supporting her as much as telling her how he could have done it better. By now he had finished his little dissertation, which I was not sure had ever reached a point, and with a sigh from the teacher we were finally getting back on track. Just like Cat Stevens' morning, the waters had broken and we were on our way up the birth canal without a paddle.

After the early labor red herring had been duly dealt with, the teacher led us into more familiar territory, even for the men. Next up for discussion was the subject of contractions: How often? How long? How painful? How to cope? Almost every man knew about contractions because women who had already been through childbirth went on about them *all* the time. They were the universal yard-stick of comparison for pain and were frequently thrown at men as a dismissive counter to our own claims of agony.

"Oh, stop your whining," a woman will say when her man has caused some form of self-inflicted injury, usually associated with having been forced to do some work around the house. "It's nothing compared to a contraction, I can tell you. Stop being a baby."

The more interesting and less well-known fact was the purpose of the contractions. Most men considered them to be the process by which the woman pushed the baby out, which eventually they indeed were. But it transpired that much work needed to be done before this could happen. Their most important job was to "open the cervix" until it was wide enough for the baby to pass through, which seemed sensible enough. They would stretch it from about the size of a key-hole to a four inch gap. Not much you may say, but apparently, this is about as easy as prying opening a safe with a plastic fork. Or, as my wife would later describe it, like pulling your bottom lip over your head. Moses probably had an easier time of it with the Red Sea. So presumably, that was what all the shouting and screaming was about? All on my own, I had worked out this process was likely to take some time.

"Whatever you women may have heard about quick labor — forget it," our charming hostess informed us. She was lucky that everyone who turned up to her classes was already pregnant, as she was proving to be a superb form of contraceptive.

It also explained why she had asked for the fees for the full set of classes to be paid in advance, because if it was pay-as-you-go, many of us would have gone by now. A few of the Moms-to-be had expressions on their faces that seemed to ask whether it was too late to give the baby back.

"Labor is likely to take a minimum of six hours, and probably a lot longer than that," the teacher opined. "So be prepared."

Six hours. That was a long time. My mind started to wander as to all the things you could do in six hours. Before I knew it, my mouth had taken over the thought process.

"Good news, boys. Enough time for 18 holes."

I think it was safe to say that none of the women present, and especially the teacher, were golfers. My comment went down about as well as someone's waters breaking on a crowded bus on a hot day. A couple of the men valiantly tried to suppress giggles as their partners glared at them, almost daring them to show any sympathy to my suggestion. Although the glazed expressions on a couple of faces revealed that they were already dreaming of the first fairway. My putting would also benefit from a few contractions to stretch the cup by about four inches.

I began to wonder how the tea-bags had gotten to look so well used as we still hadn't been allowed a break. And we had just learned even the water got that much. We had gone through early labor and without pausing for breath, we had now moved on to "active labor." The contractions would be getting longer and closer together. And of course they would be more painful. Once again we were reminded that although the symptoms were speeding up, this was still likely to be a very lengthy process.

This woman never missed an opportunity to reinforce to everyone how long everything was going to take and how much everything was going to hurt. I could have said the same thing about her classes. I was beginning to think she was a sadist.

Having said that, we were told contractions were only lasting about one minute at this stage. I started to think about the things I could do in a minute. Luckily, pride ensured that I didn't say anything out loud this time.

Finally, over an hour into the session, a pitiful crumb of advice was being thrown to the men. After all the science and biology about labor, thankfully *without* diagrams, we were at last going to get some information on the "support" element of the whole process.

The men could get involved by offering suggestions as to ways to help alleviate any distress. We could ask whether our loved one would prefer to stand and rock gently, while we men massaged their lower back. Perhaps we could run a hot, soothing bath or suggest taking a shower. This actually sounded like reasonable advice. I always felt better after a shower, but I don't think she meant it was for me. These were things that would genuinely help and would be gratefully received. Mind you, when most men offer to give their wife a massage, there is very definitely an ulterior motive at play, which was probably how some of them ended up here in the first place.

Then of course, the teacher had to go one step too far. Her next idea was that we encouraged our partner to smile after each contraction. We should give hearty cheerleader-type comments like "one less contraction to go, darling."

So was this really her theory? Just after my wife had suffered excruciating pain like she had never believed possible, I, the person who in her mind was solely responsible for causing all this grief, should give her a big cheesy grin and tell her to do likewise? I may be stupid, but a complete idiot I am not. I would stick to running the bath, thank you very much. A badly timed suggestion from me that my suffering wife should simply grin and bear it would probably result in yet another scrotum nipping.

And in a nutshell, so went active labor. Contraction after contraction, hour after hour, until we got to "transition." Dear me, a caterpillar could become cocooned, transform into a butterfly, live a full life and die before we were even half-way through this.

What on earth was transition? Surely we went through this stage months ago? Well, at least my wife did. She transformed from being my lovely wife into being this pregnant person with more mood swings than the Glenn Miller Band. She changed from a woman very confident in her body to someone who asked every day, "am I fat?" And most scary of all, from a relatively calm person, into someone who would burst into tears at the drop of a hat for what seemed absolutely no reason whatsoever, other than being in some way my fault. About the only constant she had managed to maintain throughout the entire experience was getting annoyed at me for just about everything. I even considered this to be a good thing, as it meant I brought some dependability to her life. Please tell me there was no further metamorphosis we both had to endure.

But apparently this wasn't what was meant by transition, which turned out to be what I could only describe as the eye of the storm. This was when a woman's body made the final preparations for the onslaught of birth. Again, more advice was coming my way as to how to offer support. I hoped to God that there was no more smiling involved. Luckily not, although I was told I could breathe in front of her to try to encourage her to do the same. (Mental note: Don't eat garlic on the due date.)

I should apparently also tell her not to push, which I thought was the one word you were always *meant* to say. But no, it seemed that now was not the right time. The men were also warned that it was common for a woman to become abusive and not want to be touched. No kidding, lady. At last there was something that I actually knew already. On that basis my wife's transition was coming to the end of its fifth month.

After this we were finally hearing the bell and entering the last round. Hopefully, so was this class.

We were apparently in the "second stage" of labor and now

was the time to push. The baby would come out head first. Now if you asked me, this absolutely did NOT sound the most logical or comfortable way to do things. Weren't the feet a lot smaller than the head? Judging by those damn shoes at Mothercare, they were tiny. Perhaps it worked on the same basis as the kid who puts his head through the railings? Once it was through, there was no way it was going back. Heck, for all I knew, maybe doctors really did pull children out by their ears?

Anyway, the important fact was that once the head was in sight, the end of the marathon called birth was also in sight. This was the part I felt that I was familiar with. I had a pretty good idea of what birth was like. I could just imagine how all this was going to unfold: After all, I had seen Alien. The scene where the creature writhes around in John Hurt's stomach before finally ripping its way to freedom in a spray of blood and various other fluids. That was pretty much how I expected birth to be. It would resemble a car crash. It was awful and you didn't want to look, but you just couldn't help it.

I needed to pay particular attention to this part of the routine as I had been designated the "baby catcher." As our little bundle of joy came out of its nine-month hibernation, I was meant to be there to ensure its first experience in life was not a bungee jump as the umbilical cord snapped tight, leaving the poor little thing dangling in the breeze. Of course the drawback of catching the little bugger was that I was going to have to be much closer to the business end of proceedings than I had ever intended or wanted.

Typically, just as we came to the important part of the class as far as I was concerned, the sole focus of attention seemed to be on the woman and what was happening to her. What about me? She had gravity on her side at least, whereas I had to rely on skill and daring. What were my instructions? Where was my playbook?

Oh well, I guess I would just have to wing it on the day. At least my wife wouldn't be able to see what I was doing wrong. She would have to rely on that innate sense she used to hone in on my imperfections. I would neatly step in just in time for the grand finale and with that it was a case of mission accomplished. Ground Control: One baby caught. Fire up the cigar. Pop the champagne.

So, why didn't anyone else get ready to leave? Class dismissed guys, we were done at long last. The baby was born, our life had just irrevocably changed forever and we were bona fide Daddies. For the first time I actually seemed to be at the head of the class. But all that transpired was that I was just the first person to be wrong.

Apparently we were not done. There was still more to come, literally. How could there be more? We had already got the baby. Wasn't that the object of the exercise? The finishing line? The big prize? Not for the last time, I was back in that village where I wasn't the smartest cookie.

The teacher was saying something about stage three. No, I had heard that wrong, it was actually about the third stage, if we were going to get technical. I was going to need a third wind just to get through it. For the first time in my life I was actually craving herbal tea, just so we could have a break. What was all this about then? Did we get a slow-motion action replay or something? I had better tune in.

Oh No! Tune out! Stop. Crikey, I did not need to hear that. Surely that couldn't be right. Once someone had said it out loud it seemed obvious, but all of the men were looking equally queasy about the latest turn of events.

After the birth, there is of course the "afterbirth." Two words — good. One word — very, very bad indeed. Our lovely ladies, awash with the adrenalin of having just given birth, now had to do an encore performance with the placenta, which to me always sounded like it should be made by a Japanese car company. If anyone showed me a photo or a video, I was going to throw up.

The placenta was the baby's life-support system during pregnancy. It provided the baby with blood, oxygen, food and all the other essentials. It was like the baby having its own little Winnebago stuffed full of supplies for a nine-month trip across the country. It was therefore what was on the other end of the umbilical cord. So once the baby had come out, it was going to be getting dragged right along behind. A bit like a Green Beret and his parachute. The only thought going through my head was an overpowering need to be told that my "catching" duties had ended with the baby. *Please.*

If any of you need to know more detail about the placenta and what happens to it, I regret to say you are going to have to look it up on the internet, or go to your own classes. I, quite purposefully, did not listen to a single word of what was said. Count me in for stages one and two — my role up to there seemed fairly straightforward. But when we get to the third stage, I would be exiting stage left, if it was all the same to you. A man had to know his boundaries.

ᚖᚖ

As I mentioned earlier, probably what I considered to be the most entertaining and educational part of the classes was simply the other attendees. People are fascinating, which was why chairs at French cafés all point out toward the street, so that you could unashamedly watch the passers by.

To break up the tedium of the more technical aspects of the classes, or more likely to compensate for the fact that pregnant women have to go to the bathroom on an alarmingly frequent basis, conversation often turned to more general topics about actually raising the child, once we had learned how to give birth to it.

One of the subjects of greatest debate was the issue of co-sleeping: Now obviously pre-natal class was not a good forum to talk about adultery. What I mean is, whether parents should have their child sleeping in the same bed as them, or whether the baby should instantly and always sleep in its own crib.

The first worry is that while sleeping you will roll over onto your baby and squash it, a feat that would be somewhat easier for me than for others. All I could say to that was whenever I tried to roll over onto my wife, she sensed it in an instant and dispatched me back to my side of the bed. So I couldn't see any danger from that.

Another concern was that once your baby gets into the habit of sleeping with you, you would never be able to break it. I was not sure I agreed with that either, as friends who had never allowed their child to sleep with them when a baby, said that by the time a kid turned about four years old, it automatically wanted to sleep with them anyway, citing anything from bad dreams to monsters under the bed as an excuse.

On the plus side, if your wife was breastfeeding, it would seem to make sense to have the baby as close by as possible. It had to be more disturbing for both partners if a crying baby had to be collected from its crib and brought to its food source, rather than having it on tap.

Firstly, the baby was going to cry for longer until it got what it wanted, which meant that there was more chance I would be woken up. And secondly, once I was awake, there was a large probability I would be the one dispatched to collect the little pest. On that basis, I was all in favor of co-sleeping, if that was what my wife wished.

So this was where the some-people-are-just-odd factor came in. One woman declared with great conviction that her baby would be sleeping in a separate room from the get-go. Fair enough, nothing wrong with that at all if that was your choice. Until she cited the reason behind her decision.

It transpired that she was a dog owner. When they were puppies, she let them sleep on the bed with her. Naturally, they got to like this arrangement and showed zero inclination to return to their baskets, even as they grew bigger and started to dominate the nocturnal real estate. Attempts at "tough love" had failed, with the dogs whining and pining outside the bedroom door the entire night until allowed readmission. So to this day, they still shared the marital bed, which meant there simply wasn't room for a baby as well. Yes, that's right, the dogs were getting top billing and staying in the bed. The baby, presumably, would be in the kitchen in the dog basket. And the scary thing is, it was getting a dog that required a license.

In an effort to try to glean any sort of positive from this revelation, all I could say was it proved beyond any doubt that in parenting, absolutely anything goes. They were our kids and we could raise them any damn way we pleased. You do it your way, and I'll do it mine.

It was also reassuring to discover that while I was aware that I knew absolutely nothing about raising a child, there were evidently a few people who had even less of a clue. If they could do it, then surely I could do it.

However, I was confident enough that I would do a multitude of ridiculously stupid things with my child, so I didn't consider it necessary to plan some in advance. We would be co-sleeping and that was fine with me. I had been told already that the "sexual blackout period" would be lasting at least another few months after the baby was born, so why shouldn't it be in the bed with us? It wasn't like it was going to be interrupting the making of its sibling or anything like that. I believed in sharing the spoils. If I wasn't going to be able to play with my wife's breasts, then by all means let the youngster have a go.

It also meant we wouldn't need to go back to the dreaded Mothercare to get some of those baby intercoms that were more expensive than short-wave radio transmitters. Just as well, as in my view they did the exact opposite of what they were intended for.

The principle was that they transmitted any noise your baby was making in its own room into yours, so that you knew when assistance was required. Great idea you say. Or was it? All was well and good when you could hear a constant gurgling sound coming from the monitor, or a plaintive little cry when the baby had woken up and needed feeding.

But what happened when it went quiet? The monitor was doing its job and informing you that nothing was happening. In theory, there was nothing at all to worry about. But instead, everything stops. First you pick up the monitor and shake it to see if it is still working properly. Then you put it up to your ear and demand total silence while you strain to try to make out the faintest whisper or breath. Nothing. You wait. Surely in a second there would be some sort of noise? A sniffle or a squeak; a tiny little cough; perhaps just a rustle of little bedclothes. Nothing. It has been over a minute now, what has gone wrong? Brain damage from lack of oxygen can start in less than three minutes with infants. The growing magnetic force pulling you toward the baby's room becomes overpowering and you can't help but go to see what is wrong.

Of course nothing is wrong. Junior was fast asleep without

a care in the world. Being tiny and with nostrils the size of pin-heads, it just hadn't learned to snore with the decibel factor a man of Dad's experience could muster. So you go back to your room and lie awake the rest of the night, waiting for the next ominous silence.

So, the baby was going to be sleeping with us once it was born. A decision I actually would have agreed with had I been consulted.

Just as well then that my wife was going to go through this phase of nymphomania during her pregnancy, so that I could get it all out of my system beforehand, if you'll excuse the expression.

LETTER TO DAD

Dad, I have to say I'm pretty bored in here now. All I can do when I'm not sleeping is to think about things. I've just got so many questions I want to ask you I hardly know where to start. Where should I start Dad?

For example: I know I'm only a baby, but I can't understand why if it only took you about a minute to create me, how come Mom needs the best part of a year to finish the job?

Is Mom a bit slow? Or were you just an idiot for getting stuck with her? If my mother or father, or even worse both of you, are less than clever, does that mean I'm going to be a bit dim as well? Is it my fault? Is it because of me that you two had to get together in the first place? Am I the result of a drunken Christmas party?

What's Mom like? All I know is that I'm in her tummy and I have been for more than six months. So I'm guessing she must be pretty huge then, huh?

Dad, are you ugly? Is that why you ended up with the fat girl that's a bit dense? Were you two the only ones left at the end of the school Prom and you just kind of got thrown together by a process of elimination?

That's why Mom drinks isn't it? Has she become an alcoholic because she had to settle for the ugly guy? Come on, you can't deny it, not to me. I live right next door to her bladder and that thing is full all the time. You won't believe how it encroaches on my living space, which wasn't much to start with. I have to lean on it really hard and that seems to release some cork so it can all drain out. But soon enough, it's full again. Can't you get her off the bottle? It can't be good for her if she's pregnant. Or me for that matter. It's hardly responsible now is it? I hope she doesn't drive. Maybe with a bit of luck the seat doesn't go back far enough and she can't squeeze her big belly in front of the steering wheel. That would probably be safest for everybody.

Oh My God. Will I be ugly and fat and stupid? That's why it's so dark in here, isn't it? No windows, let alone any mirrors or reflective surfaces. If I saw myself, I'd be too embarrassed to come out, whether the landlord sent in his cronies or not. I've already got this oversized head to deal with.

Dad, there's something else I need to ask you, and I need a fairly quick answer. How do I get out of here? I can see a small light down the end of the corridor, but the door doesn't look very big. A month or so ago I was pretty confident I would get out easily, but with this news about being fat and all, I'm starting to get a bit concerned. I don't want to end up being the prover-bial kid with his head stuck through the railings.

I *am* a kid right? We've established I'm not a fish or a monkey, but could I be some sort of household pet? That's not a cat flap down there is it?

CHAPTER 12

NESTING

M Y WIFE AND I come from different ends of the planet and we have lived and worked in four separate continents, so we have managed to amass quite an array of crap. We have built up a load of furniture, artwork and assorted junk that we very much like and which now adorns our apartment. In fact, we have such an assembly of items that when house-hunting, we could dismiss most places without hesitation as being too small. This was not only because we had a lot of things, but also because we seemed to have cornered the market in particularly large pieces that didn't fit into building elevators or any type of old house which had quaint little doors and low ceilings.

Having said all that, I in no way intend to make it sound luxurious, decadent or remotely boastful. We were by no means rolling in it. The expression "one man's trash is another man's treasure," could not be more fitting for the two of us. We truly did treasure the trash that we had collected, probably most of all because we had chosen it together. We were happy with our lot and had much to be thankful for, when we weren't complaining about things.

Imagine my surprise therefore, when I discovered that

almost overnight, my wife had determined that our home-sweet-home had suddenly become a tiny, squalid, filthy, dangerous, nexus-of-all-evil, that no two self-respecting, responsible parents-to-be could ever consider bringing any child into, let alone a newborn baby.

The "self-respecting and responsible" description in this instance solely refers to my wife. With reference to me, it was purely used as an expression and has no factual basis whatsoever. I have never claimed to be either and my wife has certainly never credited me with being either. She of course, qualifies with ease on both counts.

Even though I had never considered that I had come close to gaining a level of understanding of my wife's utter lunacy over the past six months or so, she definitely seemed to have raised the bar with this one. Had we quietly slipped into a parallel dimension during our slumber? In my opinion, which admittedly counted for little even on a good day, our apartment was identical to how it had been a few short months, weeks, or even days ago, when my wife was just as pregnant. Yet again it transpired that I was sadly mistaken.

In a rare outburst of sanity my wife explained the problem to me. She was "nesting." As she got closer to D-day, or to me more exact, B-day, her maternal instincts were telling her our home, sorry nest, had to be suitably prepared for the arrival of our little chick, I mean baby.

It turned out that she had decided our house was a veritable death-trap for an infant and we were going to have to make some changes — an awful lot of changes. Once again, I had been sucked into another new dimension in the wonderful world of pregnancy.

It also rapidly became clear that as my wife actually had a reason for this latest outburst, however flimsy or nonsensical, this meant that the prospect of my arguing the case was a complete non-starter.

This differed from the many times recently when she openly admitted she had no idea why she said or did anything, not that her admission had much sway in the outcome of the other arguments. If she could actually come up with a plausible reason, then of course she must be right, and of course she must be obeyed.

Obviously this had all come as a great surprise to me. No doubt other women would tell me that was probably a direct result of my not having bothered to read any of the books on the subject of pregnancy. These books would have explained to me in crushingly boring detail how "nesting" was a perfectly normal phase of pregnancy and should be welcomed with open arms, rather than my preferred choice of greeting it with fear and futile resistance.

After all, this apparently was one of the first real signs that the birth was finally not far away. This was the mother starting to make the last preparations for the impending arrival. Just as a bird builds a nest in a tree (a somewhat precarious choice considering baby birds aren't instantly born with the ability to fly, I have always thought), so does a mother want to completely rearrange her home in the most illogical fashion to make space for a baby that can barely move, and whose only comparison is a one-foot-square room with no windows. I couldn't imagine how our baby could possibly be disappointed with its new home, just as it was.

I would also like to challenge the validity of these theories in the books that I have not read. I believe that I am entitled to do that on the principle that I haven't been to the Sahara Desert, but I know it's hot. Unlike me, my wife had read countless books on pregnancy and childbirth and could probably write one that would be a heck of a lot more instructional and useful than this.

However, where do we draw the dividing-line between expectation and action? What's the difference between cause and effect? Does the relevant book tell you what to expect, or how to behave?

What I'm getting at is this: Was my wife "nesting" because it was a totally natural instinct and she couldn't stop herself even if she wanted to; or was her subconscious telling her that she should be nesting because she had read all these books and they said that was what a woman should be doing at this stage of her pregnancy? It was not as if her mind was at its strongest to resist these subliminal suggestions. It was the proverbial chicken and egg conundrum.

My view was that she shouldn't have read the books in the first place. Then she would be living in the same blissful ignorance that I was and would have no earthly idea that she needed to nest. More importantly, we would both be living in a home that didn't need to be up-rooted.

There was also the peer pressure factor. Other pregnant

women that were a little further along, or new Moms for whom pregnancy was still a vivid memory, would of course ask my wife whether she was nesting yet. Worse still, they would suggest that the mere action of her taking her tea cup back to the kitchen sink, rather than leaving it by the computer as she usually did, was a definite sign that the nesting stage was indeed upon her.

This was a tough group to resist or disappoint. No woman wanted to make it appear her pregnancy wasn't going exactly according to schedule. Or that she was in some way tardy in an important stage of the child's natural development. Once the suggestion was out there that she either was nesting, or most certainly should be, then it was a done deal.

From some of the things my wife wanted changed, I could only presume she was going to give birth to a telekinetic child. Pictures on walls and vases on tables were now weapons of mass destruction. A child just looking in their direction would apparently be enough to bring them crashing to the floor on the exact spot where the baby would be lying. Everything would have to be nailed or glued down to prevent this from happening.

We would also need to find a spherical furniture shop. As of that moment, corners had been outlawed. Even though a baby can't walk for the best part of a year, every chair, table or couch that had a corner on it was in fact a dagger in disguise that would pierce the heart of our defenseless little child. The closest suggestion I could think of as meeting the requirement for spherical objects was a pool table. It was not a well-received observation.

We had a bronze statue, bought together on a trip to Italy, which I could barely lift because it had been attached to a large marble base. Not any more, it seemed. Now it was evidently balanced precariously on the head of a pin, ready to plummet to the ground. It could fall at any second, no doubt the very same second when the baby — miraculously crawling at the age of three weeks — was passing by underneath.

The same was true of the hi-fi speakers, which my wife said should carry a government health warning. The pins on which they stood, when Baby Superman lifted the four-foot monsters off the ground, could cause untold damage. And Oh My God, those wires. Our baby would be found swinging from the back of the speaker within days, garroted by the coaxial cable. The next music we would be listening to would be coming from the prison P.A. system as we sat incarcerated for life for negligent homicide of an infant.

I did suggest covering the entire house, inside and out, in bubble-wrap as a precautionary measure. My wife gave me one of those withering looks that told me exactly how stupid I was, while at the same time asking why she ever married me.

"Well how would the baby be able to breathe?" she asked.

It was somewhat worrying that she had actually thought I was making a serious suggestion.

The undoubted highlight of all this madness though, was the attention my wife gave to a certain bookcase. To the casual observer, this looked like any other ordinary bookcase, allowing for our criteria of it being unnecessarily large: It was made of wood; it had a bunch of shelves that held books of varying shapes and sizes; it possessed a few small drawers to put keepsakes in; and it sat quietly up against a wall so as to keep it out of everybody's way. All in all, it was totally unremarkable.

So who could have known that this seemingly harmless cocktail of ingredients, when mixed together, conjured up the very spirit of all things ungodly. We were going to need an exorcism, or perhaps even Buffy the Vampire Slayer, if she had made it out of Mothercare alive. Otherwise, our child would be doing Linda Blair impersonations, spinning her head through 360 degrees and projectile vomiting pea soup everywhere. (This is pretty much what I thought all babies did anyway.)

My wife had decreed that before any child could be brought into this world, and more importantly into our home, the demonic bookcase had to go. It had to be expunged from our very existence. No matter that the books and photos would be condemned to a life of poverty on the floor; it mattered not that this was yet another huge piece of furniture that was not going to go anywhere without a fight; it wasn't relevant that we were so far from anything approaching reality that it had gotten plain silly.

The bookcase was genuinely so big that the top layer of shelves had already been sawn off when we had moved house the last time a mere two years ago, so this was going to be no easy task. Luckily, while my do-it-yourself skills were extremely limited, like most men, if I did have an area of talent it was in the field of *de*-struction rather than *con*-struction. So, in my best Tim-the-Tool-Man-Taylor fashion, I set about this book-case with gusto. I had all the necessary tools: Garlic, a cross, holy water and silver bullets.

Despite risking my very soul to eternal damnation, I managed to eventually dismantle the demonic portal, or probably more accurately, to quite comprehensively destroy it. Once decimated, its remains were summarily removed from the premises, leaving no trace of the evil it carried. I did draw the line at my wife's request for having them burned and the ashes spread over the four corners of the compass.

Having got through this task, and many others that I can assure you were of a similarly dubious nature, there was only one level of ridiculousness we had not succumbed to. That would be my wife's realization that there was simply so much wrong with our current abode, tainted as it had been by the dreaded bookcase, that the only viable alternative was to move house altogether and get a new, undesecrated living space that was pure and good and bookcase-free.

Inevitably, we duly succumbed to the utmost level of ridic-ulousness. At eight months pregnant, by which time my wife was openly complaining she was actually as big as a house, we were looking for somewhere new to live. I was sure it didn't help with the financial negotiations that it was plainly evident to everyone we were a couple who could not afford to wait forever for the right price. Even the dumbest of realtors were not going to have the wool pulled over their eyes by my nonchalant "Oh, we're just looking, no rush." However, even the brightest amongst them was undoubtedly perplexed as to why the first question my wife always asked of any potential abode was "does this place have any bookcases?"

At least we didn't have to go through any inane conversations that began with the remark, "so, why are you guys looking for a new house then?"

Luckily, we found somewhere nearby that was absolutely ideal. It fulfilled all of my wife's nesting criteria and was bigger and better laid out than our current apartment. We both knew we wanted it the second we laid eyes on it. Amazingly it was even cheaper than where we were living now, so the decision was relatively quick and simple.

Moving was neither.

At the best of times, moving can be a stressful experience. At least we had a head start in that there were no tears needed to be shed over the usual heart-wrenching trauma of leaving an old and much-loved home. A few prayers were muttered, some candles were burned as a ritual offering to the Gods lest the evil spirits had seen one of our Change of Address cards, and we got the hell out of Dodge. Or was it that we dodged out of hell? I can't remember.

I had no intention of doing the actual moving myself, but that does not necessarily mean that it was any easier. The movers, despite their years of experience, have still failed to realize that pieces of furniture are not simply pieces of furniture to their owners, with no feelings. They are living and breathing members of the family, much like pets, and need to be treated accordingly. Now this doesn't mean my wife wanted the coffee table transported in a basket, but she flinched every time a piece of furniture was roughly treated in any way, as if she too was sharing the pain.

She was convinced that everything we owned was going to be ruined. She did have a point, in that this moving company did not work on the principle of "slow and careful," but rather "how quick can we get this done and how much value can we knock off these possessions?"

Perhaps it was their way of getting revenge for the fact that everything we owned was at least 50 percent bigger and heavier than it needed to be. Furniture that wasn't antique certainly looked a lot closer to it when these guys were done. They made more chips than Frito-Lay, both to the furniture and the walls. The only thing I could say in their favor was that they had at least softened some of those dangerous corners my wife was so worried about.

Naturally, it was raining the day we moved. You couldn't tell that from the sound of the raindrops beating down on the roof of the moving truck though, because it didn't have one. Apparently no one had told them it was going to rain that day. Luckily, they had enough cling-film wrap to protect one whole sofa, almost in its entirety, even if they did the wrapping of the sofa outside, while it was already getting wet.

I could clearly see my wife's tears running down her cheeks along with the rain, so I tactfully got her back inside and making cups of tea for people who didn't want them. It was one of my few smart moves.

On my return to check out what the moving guys were

doing outside, I discovered that one of the men loading the truck was standing on our coffee table, presumably for better leverage. If my wife had seen him there, the coffee table would have had to go to the same grave as the recently departed bookcase. To his credit though, from this higher viewpoint, he was an expert in arranging the furniture so as to get the minimum amount possible onto the truck. A quick check of the small print revealed I was paying by the truckload. Or was it simply that I was paying a truckload?

Some polite comments and suggestions from me ensued, followed by a barrage of four-letter words and finger-pointing, which seemed to be a language they understood better. In the nick of time, before my wife reappeared with a cup of tea that I didn't want either, the furniture was stacked efficiently on the back of the truck, no one was standing on it, it had just about stopped raining, and we were ready to go.

So, against all the odds, we had managed to move into our new house, still as a group of two, rather than already a family of three. My wife could now safely give birth, knowing her child was going to be brought home to a brand new, shiny nest.

Perhaps our new apartment would also be warm and cozy enough to prove to be a "love-nest" and prompt the onset of the phase in my wife's pregnancy when she became a complete nymphomaniac. By this late stage, I would have ripped apart a rotten old bookcase for that every day of the week.

LETTER TO DAD

Dad, the rotten old landlord has served me with an eviction order, so I'm going to be coming out any day now. I hope you're ready.

I'm going to need help when I arrive as I have this really big bag with all my stuff. It's so heavy I can't even carry it myself. I have to pull it around on this long cord.

I'm starting to get very excited about seeing you. But how will I recognize you? Can you wear a carnation in your lapel or something? I don't want to pop out and develop an instant bond with the first guy I see, only to discover that he's the doctor and you were outside pacing the corridor smoking a cigar. You'd better be there to catch me. And let me warn you now, I seem to be greased up like I'm about to swim the English Channel, so make sure you don't drop me. It seems evident I'm going to be mentally challenged as it is with you two as parents, so the last thing I need is to be bounced on my head on day one.

Also, whatever else you do, please do not cry. I don't want to hear any of this "I'm a modern man in touch with my feelings" rubbish. Forget about all that new era sensitivity stuff, just be a real man. I'm sure Mom is going to be bawling her eyes out, so we need someone to keep up appearances.

Talking of Mom, tell her to make sure those boobs are nice and full because I'm likely to be thirsty. Don't worry about giving me a bath, just latch me straight onto that puppy with the brown nose and I'll be happy enough.

Oh, and one more thing. Kindly convey to the doctor that

if he slaps me on the butt, I'm going to piss all over him. (And as you know, I have been practicing for months now, so I won't miss.) It's the 21st century for goodness sake, we don't need to be using that kind of archaic behavior any more. And don't let him dangle me by my ankles like he's just caught a fish and wants his picture taken. I'm not Achilles.

No, seriously, I'm not called Achilles am I? You haven't gone and named me after a fruit or something ludicrous have you? You've had nine months, you must have come up with something decent by now, even if you are a bit less than intellectual. Please tell me you and Mom aren't famous and I have to get lumbered with a ridiculous name. Because I'll put myself up for adoption if you have. I mean that's just intolerable cruelty right there. Even if you didn't want me, there's no need to take it out on me. None of this is my fault, remember.

Anyway, I still have to pack and get in a good night's sleep. Tell Mom to hurry up and get that door working properly, as it doesn't look like it's been used in ages. I know for a fact that you haven't popped in to come and visit, Dad. Not to worry, I'll come to see you. I can't wait to meet you both.

CHAPTER 13

CONSPIRACY THEORY

DISCLAIMER: CAN I POLITELY ask that any women reading this book simply skip this chapter and move right along to the next one, which is the actual labor.

Honestly, I'm doing you a favor by asking and you will thank me for it later, even though you won't know why. Should you make the foolish mistake of not heeding my warning, then by the end of this chapter you will be kicking yourself and saying: "For once a man was right. I should never have read this."

I also ask in the spirit of kindness, as the last thing I would want to do is in any way lessen or spoil your appreciation of my book. How about looking at it this way? All the interesting stuff about the birth itself that you girls want to read is waiting for you in the very next chapter. Consider this as saving you time and speeding you along to the really good part. Look upon these few pages as a harmless aside for the benefit of us guys. A small detour of merriment for men, who, as you know, can't concentrate for more than about 15 minutes on anything other than sport. This is nothing more than a fabrication to smooth the bruised egos of the boys, who by now are fast realizing how pitiful their role is in the great wonder that is creation.

☙

O.K. Men — Now that I've gotten rid of the women, it's time to give you the real skinny on this whole childbirth experience as I see it. I have to confess that what I am about to share with you I have not been able to prove in any form of clinical test. But let's just say there's an overwhelming amount of circumstantial evidence to back up my theory.

This may well come as a rude shock. The information I'm about to provide should be kept locked away in the inner sanctuary of manhood; hidden in the depths of your memory vault where you keep those embarrassing things you did as a boy that you've never told anyone about. This is highly classified and extremely sensitive information. It must never, even under the most cruel and unusual torture, be revealed to the fairer sex. Wars have been fought over less.

Here in these next few pages is the exposé, the damning truth, the secret that every woman has tried to conceal throughout history. This is the clandestine pact that binds women to each other in a way that men can neither breach nor understand. A shared burden of confidentiality that unites them all in covering up the greatest conspiracy the world has ever known or will ever see.

What one single thing could be so monumental? I hear you ask, probably with some trepidation. Could women really be this devious to have maintained their silence through the centuries, without anyone ever breaking ranks? And what on earth does it have to do with having a baby?

Well, hopefully with your curiosity suitably piqued, I shall reveal everything to you. And once you know my theory, you will agree that as secrets go, this one has to rank right up there with "who shot J.R.?" and "where are the weapons of mass destruction?"

So here it is, revealed with the shock and awe that only the truth can ever bring to bear.

Childbirth doesn't hurt.

Incredible isn't it? I was amazed myself when the revelation first seeped into my consciousness, and I had to concede that the unthinkable was not merely thinkable, but was indeed a reality. It was a hard truth to take, as no one likes to admit to having been duped, fooled, swindled and taken advantage of. Well actually, most men quite like being taken advantage of, but that's a story for another day.

Men have been victim of the biggest con trick ever. Actually, maybe only the second-biggest for those poor few misguided husbands out there who still believe in the myth that after the wedding day their wife will still wear stockings and garter belts or give them a blow-job ever again.

Women have been hood-winking us for centuries into believing that bearing a child is the single most excruciatingly painful experience any human being can go through. So painful, we are told on countless occasions, that the task is only given to women. Mere men would not be able to survive it.

And because of this incredible sacrifice women make on behalf of the future of our species, men have to suffer the ultimate guilt, the consummate shame and overbearing feelings of inadequacy that manifest themselves in our subservience to women and our acquiescence in allowing them to treat us like crap the entire time.

You are probably still sitting there in total disbelief, which I can completely understand. But I imagine that I now have the complete and utter attention of the male fraternity. Also, I can safely predict that any woman who read past the disclaimer at the top of the chapter has certainly stopped reading by now, and quite possibly tested the aerodynamic qualities of this book. If any have soldiered on, I would guess it's a few first-time Moms-to-be who have not yet been invited into the inner circle of knowledge and are secretly hoping that my claims are true. After all, this isn't information that a woman needs until she is pregnant, when the pretence has to begin.

I'm also sure you men now understand why I insisted the women didn't read this. Once they know that we know, once they realize that the game is up, the whole balance of power will be irrevocably shifted. The Status Quo — and by that I mean the situation, not the seventies rock band — will be destabilized and could even bring about women's worst fear: The dawn of a new male era.

It is truly mind-boggling. Having made this discovery, in some small way I realized how the primitive man must have felt when he created fire for the first time; how proud Newton must have been when he discovered gravity; how McDonald's must have rejoiced when they came up with the drive-through.

The first reaction is denial. But when you begin to analyze things, the fog of deception clears and it all slowly starts to make sense. Just think about the facts for a minute.

Childbirth is the one thing women can do that men can't. And by that I mean the one thing they can do by design, according to the laws of Mother Nature. I'm not talking about acquired abilities such as talking for hours on end on the phone without even drawing breath; buying a little black dress/shoes/bag, to go with the four other little black dresses/shoes/bags that they already have; redecorating your house when you weren't looking; Telling all of their friends, close or otherwise, the inner-most secrets of your sex life together, which basically means a list of your failings.

Anyway, the point I'm trying to put across is that women can make any claim they like about childbirth, safe in the knowledge that men can never go through the experience to discover the real truth. We can therefore never challenge the version of events that the women have handed down to each other through the ages. It is exclusively their version of the story that we have to listen to.

But let us look a little more closely at some of those facts. Childbirth is a completely and gloriously natural phenomenon. It is at the core of our very existence, no less. It is not a medical operation in the sense that something is being fixed that is wrong in some way. Women have been designed for this. Indeed you could possibly go so far as to say it is their singlemost important function. Even more than shopping. So, given all that, why on earth would it be agony?

The only other functions we all share that, like childbirth, are a necessity for the continuation of our species, are eating and sex.

Does eating hurt? Do we suffer the throes of agony every time we have a meal? No. Perhaps after a particularly dodgy curry or a dubious Mexican burrito, we may well be a victim of some temporary discomfort, but on the whole, eating is a pleasurable experience. Of course it is, because it is vital to our staying alive.

The same goes for sex. Unlike food, we certainly, and unfortunately, don't base our needs on the three-square-a-day principle. But I think we can all agree that sex is a joyous occasion. OK, "barely" may well be my wife's response, but I think you get the idea of what I'm trying to say. A minority of people may get up to some rather kinky stuff that involves leather, shackles and pain, but they will tell you that they like it that way, so it doesn't count as being painful in a negative sense.

My point is that the activities that are essential to life are made to be enjoyable, to ensure that we keep doing them and therefore continue to exist as a species. On that irrefutable logic alone, it simply doesn't make any sense that childbirth would hurt.

Back when we humans were living in caves, because there was no cable, the men would go out hunting during the day. The women would stay back at the rock and sit around the fire, chatting amongst themselves and cooking the animals that we had killed.

Unfortunately, that was also when they learned about making fur coats. Oh yes, even back then the women had caught onto the idea of expensive clothing. Men managed to get some degree of revenge by pretending that mink was the smoothest fur of all. I mean let's face it. Did Mr. Hunter-Gatherer really want to risk death taking on a grizzly bear so that his wife could look good? Or would he rather go and beat the crap out of a dozen or so stinky little rodents and have done with it?

Anyway, the point was the men were always out foraging, which meant they were never around to witness the birth of their children.

As an aside, it's easy to see why modern men need to go out at the weekend and play golf. It's a primal urge that's very hard to resist and is a subconscious memory of being out in the bush swinging a club all those centuries ago.

After a hard day of mink killing, the men simply arrived back at El Cave sometime after dark to discover that (A) He was apparently late, even though he hadn't invented a watch yet and hadn't said what time he would be back. And (B) Junior had mysteriously arrived during his absence. Then, over a rack of ribs, the men would have to sit and listen to the tales of the screaming and the wailing, the pain and the suffering his loyal and selfless woman had gone through in order to bring his child into the world. And this would be a story that had more re-runs than "Friends."

Now we are in the modern era, the pretence has become more difficult to perpetuate. So, the women have had to take their deception to a much higher level. Hospitals, for example. Why do women need to go to a hospital to have a baby? They never used to, because, as stated above, this was a perfectly natural procedure, not a medical complication. Why does a woman's mother almost invariably turn up a week or so before the birth, be it from down the street or the other side of the world? Because as the mother, it was her responsibility to ensure her daughter dutifully continues the myth of childbirth.

I was born at home, and as far as I can recall, I was the only one crying. My mother had even confessed that giving birth to me hadn't hurt. (See, I told you I'd revisit it.) However, as we have developed drugs for just about everything, the easiest way to give credence to the theory that something is really painful is to administer drugs. And the bigger they are, the better.

Once again, the women incorporate some clever gender separation to avoid us men working out exactly what was going on here. Hands up any guy who has been given an epidural. Not many, I'm guessing. Why was that? This was meant to be a kick-ass pain-killer drug, the only one that could numb the senses during such excruciating agony. So, how come men had never been allowed to have it during an operation? An epidural is administered in the lower spine and is an anesthetic block that can affect the upper abdomen down to the lower extremities. So what was so special about that? Why couldn't men have one? There was probably a bunch of sportsmen out there that could have benefited from one of those. Well if you ask me, the only reason we were not allowed an epidural is because it was all part and parcel of the myth that women have created.

"Oh no Sir, no male injury could be sufficiently painful that you would need an epidural. Here, take an aspirin for that broken leg and be a brave boy about it. Goodness me, it's not as if you are having a baby."

Another problem of modern-day life is the sheer number of us. Again, back in the caves, the women had all day to talk in total privacy, so they could explain to their daughters the secrets of the childbirth conspiracy. They could tell them there was nothing to worry about, that childbirth was like falling off a log. Then it would be stressed to them that their most important responsibility was to keep the men believing that birth was the most incredibly difficult and agonizing experience, for which women deserved undying gratitude and obedience — and a fur coat.

Skip forward to the modern day and there were simply too many of us around for any chance of uninterrupted schooling. Women would have to find another way to pass down the ancient teachings to protect their dark secrets.

Welcome to the world of antenatal classes. Why did we need to have classes? Yet again, I must point out that birth is a totally natural experience. Did we need classes on how to eat? Again, the answer is no. The first thing babies seemed to be able to do was to put stuff in their mouth, regardless of what it was. Nature has imprinted in us the instructions for basic survival. It was instinct. We didn't need lessons.

What about sex? A bit of a grey area I must admit, as my wife has frequently suggested some room for improvement on my part, but basically it was the same theory all over again. Did Dad have to explain to his son how to get an erection? I don't think so. Boys hit puberty and their manhood came along (or more precisely, up) like buses — never around when you needed one and then three appear in a row. Sure, arguments could be raised as to standards of performance, but in terms of just getting the job done, it was a given, with an "A" for enthusiasm.

So why was there all the fuss about antenatal classes? The answer of course was so that women could continue to pass along the commandments through which they control the world. The information was far too sensitive to be put in writing, so down through the ages it is spread by word of mouth. Why do you think women are always talking to each other? To make the pretence all the more compelling, they even go so far as to invite men to some of the classes, knowing full well, we will not be able to attend every class, because they were cunningly scheduled when sporting events were on, or at the weekend, when there were games of golf to be played. It was an audacious bluff, which simply goes to prove how sly and cunning they really are.

Should some men actually go to a class, they may well start to realize the validity of my theory. For example: One exercise men are encouraged to share in is to learn about breathing. Excuse me? I have been breathing all of my life and I have well and truly got the hang of it, thank you. And come to think of it, I never needed any lessons for that either. A quick slap on the bottom from the doctor immediately after I was born and I was off and running, or breathing. And I've been doing it successfully ever since.

This lesson was yet another sham. Its sole purpose was to give men the tiniest feeling of being involved. The belief we were able to support our partner and help her deal with the almost unbearable pain. As if just saying "breathe" to someone who was in agony was going to make the slightest difference. I can't believe women have got away with this pretence for so long.

Here's another thing. The next time a bloke you're playing football with gets clobbered in the cojones, try offering to help him breathe and see how it supports him through the agony. I can give you a clue — it doesn't. And anyone who suggested breathing as a remedy would most likely very swiftly need a pain cure of their own. If women are saying that breathing is a sensible way of dealing with the rigors of childbirth, then I'm saying it obviously doesn't hurt.

The reason the women of today have to go to all these classes to be able to have a baby is because they have to be taught how to fake it. They need to learn how to wail and scream and pretend that they are in agony. That is also why the majority of women always want another woman with them at childbirth. It is not for the moral support, it's more like having a prompter, someone to remind them of their lines should they forget the script.

"Ok honey, the next contraction is coming and it's going to be a big one, so brace yourself for the pain." (Wink, wink). Then they both look at the man, just in case he didn't realize where the blame lay. "Scream if you need to, we all understand." (Nudge, nudge.)

The same goes for the hospitals. A bunch of doctors, nurses and midwives all crowd around the impending mother so the father-to-be can't actually get a decent look at what was going on. They are not doing anything medical, but rather they are actually providing a barrier as good as any NFL blocking play. Then, out of Dad's view, they can coach Mom and encourage her to make all the right noises.

Any women still reading this drivel may rightly point out that a lot of doctors are men, so wouldn't the secret have come out ages ago? The problem here is that little thing they call the Hippocratic Oath. Doctors are not allowed to reveal the secrets of their patients. Now while many times that is probably a blessing, in this instance it has helped protect an evil lie.

Some women probably feel a little uncomfortable about this charade and worry that they won't be convincing. For those few there is an extra exercise to get them through. These women get told they can shout every obscenity they have ever wanted to at their husband with complete impunity. After all, he was the cause of their condition and all this imaginary suffering. How could any woman resist that opportunity? How often could a woman be given carte blanche to offload all those pent-up frustrations on her partner and have him not only stand there and take it, but actually feel guilty enough about it to want to ask for her forgiveness?

"You complete bastard. This is all your fault. You stupid jerk. Seven hours I've been in agony for the sake of two minutes of indulgence and you being so drunk you couldn't get a condom on properly. And even that attempt took longer than your main performance. You @#*!!"

Of course, the more public this high volume humiliation is, the more therapeutic for the woman. Obviously, that was just a hypothetical example and in no way should be considered to bear any resemblance to a re-enactment of anything my darling wife might have said to me.

Still, you can understand after a vitriolic attack like that, or worse, why so many men feel compelled to go out and buy those diamond earrings the wife has been nagging about for so long. How do women manage this? When did it happen that women were deserving of an expensive present for giving birth? Didn't they want the baby in the first place? Shouldn't the gift of life be more than sufficient? What present does Daddy get? These women are cunning and devious in the extreme.

☾☽

Not sure of my theory yet? OK then, here's another log to chuck on the conspiracy fire, which is burning ever brighter. Think of the occasions you have heard or read about a woman giving an emergency birth. The woman who has her baby on an airplane or in the back of a cab on the way to the hospital. Or just think about all of the poorer nations that don't even have access to all these drugs and facilities and still have their babies the old-fashioned way.

A quick aside: We had our baby in Singapore, which is renowned for having a lot of rules and regulations. My wife and I — well, my wife, really — chose to have our baby at home rather than at a hospital, where everything is sterile and impersonal. Besides, she has seen enough births at hospitals to know it wasn't what she wanted. A female colleague at my office was astounded to discover that this was even legal. I assured her that it was, which then brought her to question the wisdom of our decision.

"Why didn't you want to have your baby the traditional way?"

Moving swiftly along. In all of these instances of emergency births, when do you hear about the excruciating pain? About the wailing and the screaming? The answer is: You don't. The woman on the plane or in the cab is most likely in a mild panic and forgets her script. Also, she doesn't have her support network around her to help with the pretence. She's so worried about some complete stranger looking at her bits she forgets all about her role-play. A squeal of embarrassment is much more likely than a genuine cry of pain. Why else would a totally untrained cab driver or policeman be able to help some woman deliver her baby with such apparent ease? The whole charade starts falling to pieces around them. They have their baby totally naturally, totally drug-free, with barely a whimper or a complaint to be heard. The husband is still probably in for some abuse, but you get my drift. Of course, any women within range will rush over to help and try to shoo away all the men, fearing their secret is in jeopardy.

ை

For those few of you who are still not convinced, let's look at it from another angle. How well do women actually handle pain? That's right. Not very well at all. A broken nail; a stubbed toe; a mild headache; any one of these mishaps is enough to set off the waterworks. You would think that they at least had a compound fracture with all the histrionics going on. Compare that to men, who simply swear loudly and then move on.

Even the mere thought of pain is enough to set women off. If there's a wasp nearby and someone might get stung, they're straight into panic mode. If women were meant to be able to endure the supposedly incredible pain of childbirth, they would surely be able to deal with the minor day-to-day stuff an awful lot better, wouldn't they? I'm sorry, but the logic just doesn't add up.

Compelling isn't it? And still there's more. Know any women who have had more than one child? And by that I mean more than one birth, twins don't count. Of course, the answer is we all do. Many of us are from families with brothers and sisters, uncles and aunts.

Now how does that make any sense? Men repeatedly have been told that this childbirth lark is the single most agonizing experience known to the human race, barely survivable. If so, what are the chances women would get up, dust themselves off, and say "well, really glad that's over. I think I'd like to have another one and go through all of the excruciating pain of childbirth again please."

To compare, let me go back to what I would consider to be the nearest male equivalent of unbearable pain — a solid whack to the groin. Men have not, do not, and will not ever get up gingerly to their feet and exclaim:

"Wow! That was a really beautiful experience, totally empowering. I feel much more of a man now, I can hardly wait for it to happen to me again. It will probably be even better the second time, I imagine."

It is such an awful experience, that even thinking about it can bring a tear to the eye and cause our undercarriage to retract involuntarily. I would go as far as to say we would even rather go shopping with our wife on a Saturday afternoon than go through a repeat performance of that particular experience. That, ladies and gentlemen, is the definition of what real pain is. It is most certainly not anything any sane person would voluntarily go through more than once.

We men have been conned. Fair enough, I'm prepared to hold up my hand and acknowledge a job well done. The girls have been pulling the wool over our eyes for centuries. But finally the game is up and the proverbial cat is well and truly out of the bag.

Childbirth is a breeze.

Women do it all the time, and when they're not doing it, they spend the majority of the time talking about doing it. It's all part of the sacred script. Whenever they are in the presence of men, they have to rehash the story of how painful it was to give Daddy the son he always wanted, until they make us so guilty we go and huddle in a corner. Then, as soon as we're out of earshot, they're all laughing their heads off that men have fallen for the oldest conspiracy in the book.

Confront them on the issue and they will deny it strenuously, of course. Their ace in the hole is that they know that we can never actually prove it, so it can only ever remain a theory. So men, it is up to us to try to spread the word. It's our mission to go forth and enlighten people to the new gospel. We have to break men free from the shackles of guilt.

And what better way to do that than to tell as many of your buddies as possible to buy this book and read the truth?

Childbirth does *not* hurt.

Of course I was never going to mention any of this to my own wife. She had almost run out of time in her pregnancy for her to sink into the depths of nymphomania. I certainly wasn't going to say anything to get me in trouble when that happened.

CHAPTER 14

LABOR

I GOT THE CALL FROM my wife that her waters had broken at about 7 p.m. as I was cycling home from work. Yes, the foolish health-kick had continued right until the bitter end. Luckily, at my wife's most recent doctor's appointment, she had weighed in still a few pounds lighter than me, so at least we had avoided the dreaded crossover.

Being on a bike, there wasn't a great deal I could do to accelerate my arrival, but I did my best Lance Armstrong impersonation and peddled for all I was worth. I turned up at home a sweaty, panting mess a good minute earlier than usual.

My wife was surprisingly calm, all things considered, which was good to see, as I would have had absolutely no idea what to do were she not. Even after the dreaded classes, "hot water and towels" was the limit of my knowledge on the subject of birth, and I didn't even know what I was meant to do with either — make tea and dry things? What little I had picked up from the prenatal classes immediately evaporated from my memory.

She was pacing around humming to herself in some sort of yoga style every time a contraction came. So far, they seemed short and mild, and nothing compared to what we had been warned to expect. I did not say that, just in case.

As stated, we had decided to have our baby at home. "We decided" meaning that my wife had informed me that was what she intended to happen and I didn't have any objections, did I? The result of that decision was that there was a checklist of tasks that had been assigned to me, probably to keep me occupied as much as anything. It was wholly unlikely I would be given any real responsibility. The biggest of these assignments was to fill the birthing pool with water. Oh yes, this was not merely to be a home birth, but also aquatic.

Now before anyone starts getting upset about the thought of babies drowning at birth, fear not. All the time a baby is in the womb, it is in fact immersed in fluid. So to be born into water is perfectly safe and in many ways, more natural than being beached and immediately subjected to a million watts of neon lighting in a hospital ward. At birth the baby was still getting everything it needed from the placenta through the umbilical cord. There was also no danger of a baby gulping down copious amounts of water with its first breath. While the umbilical remained attached for those first few minutes, a baby could still get oxygen through the cord, as it had been for the past nine months. It was quite amazing what you learned during this ordeal.

Secondly, a birthing pool was said to be considerably more comfortable for a woman in labor. The warmth of the water was soothing, while the buoyancy it provided helped alleviate some of the pain of contractions. Being in water was also said to speed up the entire process. So for someone who had chosen to give birth at home, with no drugs in sight even if screaming in agony, a spot of haste didn't seem a bad idea at all.

Not surprisingly, the birthing pool was considerably bigger than our water tank. So although I was running a hose from the shower to the pool, it didn't take long to deplete the hot water supply before it had even left a visible tide mark. Buckets of hot water (so I was right) from other bathrooms were required to supplement the process, while the tank in our bedroom reheated. Even the pitiful contents of the kettle were added to the cause.

Though the job was getting done with what I considered to be almost military precision, between contractions my wife was chastising me. Apparently it was taking too long and we should keep filling the pool with cold water if the hot had run out. While that to me seemed to defeat the purpose of the exercise, I for once realized this was not the time to argue. So I left the hose from the shower running with cold water, albeit slowly. It also now dawned on me that I was on borrowed time until I received the inevitable complaint when she got into the pool to discover the water wasn't hot enough. Yet again it was a case of "Damned if you do, damned if you don't." A situation I referred to as "everyday life."

By about 8:30 p.m. the pool was half full and still comfortingly warm. As the tank in the other bathroom replenished, additional buckets were added. But as the bucket relay slowed, it left me some time to attend to the next item on the list. Now as far as my wife was concerned, this was my most important task — candles.

Again in contrast to the harsh lighting of a hospital, the bedroom was to be decked out in candles, many of which were given to my wife by her friends for exactly this occasion. And let me tell you, this was no ordinary assortment of candles you would expect to see when there was a blackout. Oh no: We had herbal, scented and perfumed candles; we had large and small, fat and thin, round and square; there were candles on dishes or in glass vases; candles that floated or swung from a frame; candles covering every color of the rainbow or all of them in one. It was a veritable fire hazard. My only comfort was that almost everywhere you turned, there seemed to be someone wandering around with a bucket of water.

Once lit, the various aromas fought with each other for dominance. Meanwhile, commando groups of wax abseiled their way down the side of their respective candles and met up on the table to form a swirling mass like psychedelic volcanic lava.

If an outsider had taken one pace into this darkened room to be greeted by all of these candles, they would almost certainly have called Social Services or the police. At first glance, someone could easily be mistaken for thinking they had interrupted a satanic cult about to sacrifice a newborn to their God. Of course, one step further inside the room, the flickering candlelight would have revealed the "Finding Nemo" paddle pool, after which the worst of the evil imagery was somewhat dissipated.

The third item required to set the mood was music. I had failed with my suggestion of having a Jazz quartet sitting in the corner of the room. Instead, my wife had picked out some of her favorite music to relax her and help her through the tougher moments.

During our many years together, I have done my best — and with some degree of success — to re-educate my lovely wife in the world of music appreciation. That is to say, to wean her off what I considered to be the terrible crap that she used to listen to and to get her liking what I liked: Rhythm & Blues, Jazz, funk and soul. However, this was an occasion where she was drawing on her more primal instincts. I regret to report she had reverted to her old and worst musical habits. In an apparent bid to help me empathize with the pain of her contractions, I would have to suffer the agony of listening to the likes of Loreena McKennitt, who herself sounded as if she was in labor.

The aforementioned soft moans that were accompanying my wife's contractions had now become not quite so soft and were coming through at more regular intervals. They actually helped to drown out the music, so for me were almost soothing. My wife was also finding it harder to concentrate on things, such as watching TV, that were aimed at distracting her attention from the pain.

Like a professional athlete before a big race, she had started to limber up and get her mind "in the zone." It was now 9:45

p.m. and it was time to call for back-up. Luckily, our doula Vicki only lived a stone's throw away and could get to our house in about five minutes. Apart from being a fully trained nurse, she was probably also my wife's closest friend.

Being a guy, I did not take it remotely personally that my wife would rather a friend be her main support than her loving husband. In fact, it was a huge relief. As I said, my idea of what happened during childbirth was loosely based on the scene from Alien. The movies that portray actual "normal" child-births — well, even someone as stupid as me can tell you that was not even remotely credible.

So, the most I was likely to be able to add to proceedings was the pathetic encouragement of "breathe," or "push." And most likely, not even at the appropriate times. I had my job to do and cheerleader or coach was not on the list. If things started looking ugly, I intended to busy myself getting more buckets of water.

Vicki arrived, and with the benefit of all her experience she was able to tell how far along my wife's contractions were without even needing to ask her. She started barking out a few orders to the entourage that had arrived with her. Her voice had an almost schizophrenic quality: When talking with my wife she was soft-spoken, calm and reassuring; when giving out instructions to the rest of us, she did not leave the slightest doubt that she expected her orders to be carried out to the letter and instantly, so help you God.

Amazingly, I had not done everything wrong yet, so things were as much on schedule as they could be for an event that didn't have one. The other Doula-girls knew the routine and were busy being busy: Still cameras were loaded with film, digital video cameras were tested for lighting and zoom ability, and just generally played with because it was fun.

Someone was even taking notes to keep a record of the highlights. That was great news for me, as I was also meant to be taking notes for this book. Their records would allow me to concentrate on the more observational aspects, while they covered all the technical details.

Quite what conclusions anyone would have drawn had they walked in on this motley crew was beyond belief. It looked like we were making a movie as we seemed to have more extras than Ben Hur.

The fact all these women were so efficient made me feel somewhat superfluous to requirements, almost to the point of irrelevance. Childbirth was the exclusive domain of women, with the necessity of a man's role in proceedings having ended roughly nine months ago. And my contribution to the pregnancy back then had even been pretty marginal.

Everybody else knew what they were doing, except for me. Everybody including me also was well aware that I was the only one who didn't know what he was doing. In fact, that was the single thing I did know, and it wasn't helping any. Thank God we were having the baby at home, or I think I would have been asked to leave. A couple of the doula-girls were probably wondering whether they could still get away with it. What happened to the good old days when a man's role entailed nothing more taxing than pacing the corridors and lighting up a fat Cohiba when apprised of the good news? I had even been practicing that.

Perhaps after the birth, women thank their men for the priceless gift they had received. But before and especially during the birth, they just give you that askance look that says "this is *all your* fault, you did this to me; you ruined my body; you caused me this pain; and now you just stand there looking stupid."

I checked in on my wife, like a security guard patrolling his patch. She and Vicki were engaged in what appeared to be a slow waltz. Not one that was in time to the music, but then I doubted anyone had successfully danced to the current mutilation of a violin that was seeping out of the speakers. They were rocking gently back and forward in a rhythm all of their own making as another contraction hit. Each one was a bit longer and a bit stronger than the previous, like waves on an incoming tide.

By 10:30 p.m. Vicki had decided it was time to call in the doctor. We had discussed this previously, when I had stated my insistence he be called sufficiently in advance that there was not even the slightest possibility of him arriving late, however quickly events progressed. I was not sure whether this was because of my concern about having the birth without the security of a medical expert in case of emergency, or whether it was a more simplistic desire to have at least one other man amongst this bevy of women, just for moral support.

It turned out to be a fortuitous decision. He wasn't at home, so we had to leave a message on his machine. His mobile phone was switched off, so another message was left there. His paging service wasn't able to get hold of him either, but politely informed us that they had left him a message. We said it was urgent, to which they less politely informed us that that information was of course in the message. Not a great help. Visions of my own father and his growing panic at the lack of a midwife crept into my mind. At least I had all the doula-girls here, who had done this countless times before.

Nothing if not organized, Vicki was in possession of the mobile phone number of our doctor's wife. Minutes later, she finally managed to interrupt his dinner and tell him to get over here immediately. No, there was no time for dessert.

Once my wife and I (OK, mainly me) were reassured the doctor was indeed on his way, it was decided to move proceedings to the birthing pool. I was relieved by this, not because of any heartfelt desire for my wife's pain to be as minimal as possible, but because I knew the water was losing temperature every minute. The colder it got, the more grief I would get.

The warm water (crisis averted) immediately did provide a soothing effect and made my wife more comfortable. Or perhaps less uncomfortable would have been more accurate. The yoga-style moans had become distinctly louder and their pitch had dropped about half an octave. As the next contraction hit, the swearing began.

My wife had warned me that during labor she was likely to be very vocal and not exactly lady-like, so it came as no surprise to hear some bad language. For anyone who had ever been in the car when my wife was driving, they would already be impressed by the amount of restraint she had shown. A hundred yards was about the maximum distance she could get — barely into second gear — before some other motorist had been severely cursed.

And as far as the men were concerned, it was about the first thing during the whole birth experience that finally made some sense. With crying not being a popular choice among the male fraternity, a good old expletive was usually the best medicine for dealing with pain.

It was also a very good barometer to tell what type of pain someone was suffering. A quick, bullet-like "FUCK!" was indicative of a short, sharp pain, such as stubbing your toe. A long drawn out "F-U-U-U-C-K-K" demonstrated a slow-building, aching pain that would keep getting worse long after your breath had run out, such as hitting your thumb with a hammer. Your brain had enough time to relay a message to you that said, "any second, that is *really* going to hurt."

My wife's utterances were somewhere in the middle. Vicki kept talking to her quietly, offering a mix of sympathy and suitable words of encouragement. I was mute, still torn between whether this was a "push" moment or "breathe." I only had two choices and I still couldn't decide. The doula-girls whispered in the background as one of them took notes. My performance was being rated and I was quite sure I was failing to make the grade.

The next minute my wife was waving to me, so I presumed all must be well. I waved back. "You're doing great, honey," I whispered encouragingly, inane smile on my face. An impatient frown spread across hers and she waved again. The penny dropped. It was not a "Hi there" wave, but a "come over here now" wave. Having worked this out I duly obliged and went over to sit by the pool. She was still weakly flapping her hand around, so I offered her mine to hold. She grabbed on and cradled it between both her hands as if it were a cup of hot soup from which she drew comfort. This was a big moment for me. It seemed I was not only participating, but actually managing to do something useful. Of course my ability to jot down notes on the proceedings was now severely limited, but perhaps that was her intent all along?

Suddenly I got a moment of empathy as I was able to sense when the next contraction started. No, I hadn't got in touch with my feminine side, but I had noticed my hand was going a very pale white color as my wife gradually crushed it in a vice-like grip. Professional arm-wrestlers could learn a thing or two from my wife's deathly hold on my poor little hand, which was having all of the blood squeezed out of it. The low moaning sound that was pain in an audible form made a reappearance. I had to check that it wasn't me making it.

We had done an experiment in parenting class by squeezing a block of ice for a minute to get an idea of what the growing pain of a contraction was like. I began to realize it had not been a very good experiment. First of all, after practicing on an inanimate block of frozen water, my wife was now trying to squeeze my hand hard enough to make it melt, and she had almost succeeded. Secondly, if the contraction was hurting her sufficiently to make her inflict this amount of pain on her adorable husband, then the game with the ice just wasn't in the same league.

The contraction passed. My wife thankfully reverted to the soup grip and the blood flowed back into my fingers, returning them to their original shape. But, just like buses, another contraction would be along in a minute or two. My wife was now on her knees in the pool, letting the hot water soothe and support her belly. At least in my current position, I had been excused bucket duty. She rested her elbows on the edge, and leaned forward over them, letting her arms take some of the weight. She almost looked as if she were praying. Mind you, this was probably a time when a lot of women gave it a try, in between taking His name in vain.

After a few more contractions, my hand looked as if it had been in the water for a few hours, all wrinkled and creased, not to mention about half the size it used to be. As the next contraction hit and another wave of pain flooded through my wife, she leaned forward even further and drew my hand toward her as if she were going to hold it to her chest. No, we were heading higher, she was pulling it to her cheek so that I could stroke her face, or maybe she was going to kiss my hand in a sign of love and togetherness as we shared this amazing experience.

She *bit* me.

We have all seen the old movies where the hero bites down on a belt or a stick as the bad guys give them a good whipping, or as the doctor digs a bullet out of their shoulder with no anesthetic. Well, my hand was now that stick. As I realized what was happening, I tried to gently pull my hand away. My wife, to her eternal credit, and to the relief of my career as a journalist, loosened her fangs and spared my fingers any lasting damage.

If ever we needed a signal that events had moved onto another level, then this was it. It was also a sign that took about a week to wear off.

∞

As if he had been waiting in the wings for his cue, the doctor arrived. Rather than make an apology for having deprived him of his dessert, Vicki chose to welcome him with "why did you turn your phone off, Paul?" Having worked together on many deliveries — Sorry, I mean births. As I have been told more than once, delivery is for pizza — Dr. Paul took the abuse with aplomb. He scanned the room to appraise the situation and I think came to the same conclusion that had been facing me all evening. There were an awful lot of women here.

He gave me a nod of salutation that seemed to say: "I bet you're glad I'm here." He could not have been more right.

Vicki gave him a brief progress report, but being the consummate professional, he wanted it from the horse's mouth, so he asked my wife directly.

She gave a brief description of her latest contraction and said how far apart and how long she thought they were. Then she added.

"I'd like you to do a vaginal exam please."

In layman's terms a V.E. (as the pros call it) is a way for the doctor to tell how far dilated a woman is by using the most technical pieces of equipment, his fingers.

There were varying degrees of stunned-rabbit looks from around the room, myself included. It was the last thing anyone had expected my wife to ask for. A V.E. was really a guesstimate at best and didn't make any difference to proceedings. To be remotely accurate, it needed to be done during a contraction, which was of course the most painful time to do it, and may result in you not getting your fingers back. I could certainly empathize with that. It was also unreliable because things could change extremely quickly, especially for women who had already had a child. Lastly, it was an exercise in futility, because there was absolutely nothing you could do about the result anyway.

The look on Dr. Paul's face was one of trepidation, but for a completely different reason. Being a talented doctor, gifted with the powers of observation, he could not fail to have noticed that he was not in his customary birthing suite at the hospital with his client conveniently on her back, legs akimbo for ease of access. My wife was immersed in a pool full of water.

"You'll have to get in the water," Vicki said with a detectable hint of relish.

Considerately, Dr. Paul had taken off his shoes when he had arrived at the house. However, he was making no immediate moves to get his socks off or roll up his trouser legs. He didn't look like he had any intention whatsoever of getting in that water. Evidently he considered he was more than playing his part by having come to our house, rather than us to his hospital. Lines had to be drawn somewhere, and the dividing-line between dry and wet was going to be the place he made his stand.

My wife seemed to be aware of the deadlock and volunteered to stand up to make his task easier. What was so special about him? I had at no point been offered such consideration about anything. With an obvious sense of relief, Dr. Paul squeezed on a sterile glove and moved in for his examination. From where I was watching, it didn't look a particularly pleasant experience for either party, but thankfully for both, a short one.

The room fell expectantly silent as we waited for the pronouncement. For a woman to be fully dilated, which would mean the birth was imminent, she should have been around four to five inches.

"Two inches," Paul said authoritatively. The news could not have been worse if they were telling me that was my genital measurement.

This had been what I had worried about when the examination was first asked for. It meant we probably weren't even half way through this, and it didn't take a genius to work out the pain was going to get worse in the second half. I feared for my hand.

My wife had already returned to the comfort of the water, but now slumped lower, leaning on the edge of the pool with one arm, head drooped.

"Oh God. If it's only two inches, I don't think I can do this."

Everyone else was bemused. Only minutes earlier, Vicki had signaled to the other doulas her estimate that my wife was more than three inches dilated, which meant the worst was over and the birth was near. It was a sign to the rest of her troops to prepare for the final stage of the operation. Dr. Paul's words were like the General giving the order for the forces to stand down.

I knew that this was definitely neither a "breathe" nor a "push" moment, but I had no idea what else to say instead. Vicki did.

"Don't worry. You can do this. Things can change really quickly. Listen to your body, what's it telling you?"

Dr. Paul was totally confident in his judgment, which meant that as far as he was concerned, there were a good few hours to go before his services would be needed. Perhaps that had some bearing in his answer? The glove was snapped off and thrown in the bin as he disappeared into the bathroom to wash his hands. He was on his way out, probably to go back to the restaurant and get his dessert. Maybe he had ordered a soufflé, or some other delicacy that took 20 minutes to prepare?

As a couple more contractions washed over her, I could sense another change. The moan had become more of a grunt. It had more purpose, more venom. With a little effort it could have turned into a guttural scream, except it was about two octaves too low to be called a scream.

"I want to push. I want to push," my wife groaned.

Damn! A "push" moment had come along and I hadn't been ready for it. I'd missed a window of opportunity. Should I chip in with a "breathe" straight away for good measure, or were the two distinctly separate?

There was instantly a greater sense of urgency in the room. Even if I didn't know what was going on, and I surely did not, I knew something significant had occurred. Fortunately, everyone else seemed to know both what was happening and what to do about it.

Vicki dispatched one of the doula-girls forthwith to go and get the doctor back. His little disappearing trick was not going to work. It seemed he was destined never to have that dessert after all. Luckily, the elevators in our building were painfully slow and he hadn't managed to get too far before he was tracked down and summoned back to his post. If he wanted his appearance money, then he had better make one.

Meanwhile, things in the bedroom were starting to resemble and episode of Grey's Anatomy. The volume had been turned up and everyone was moving around purposefully at twice their previous speed. The quiet reverence with which everyone had tried to preserve the mood had vanished. The cast was building up for the grand finale. All except me, of course, as my hand was still a kidnap victim.

Suddenly that situation also changed as my wife released me from captivity. Once more, almost instinctively, she sensed she needed the support of a woman rather than a man. She needed someone who had experience of what she was going through, rather than someone who had merely caused it. Yet again, I felt very superfluous to requirements.

It was probably just as well. As the pace of proceedings picked up, it was becoming almost impossible for me to stay in sync. My utterings of husbandly support had been reduced to some combination of "peathe" and "brush," which weren't really a lot of use to anybody. Luckily, as everyone else concentrated on doing something relevant, my short-comings seemed to slip through almost unnoticed. There was now no doubt about it. We were having a baby.

With immaculate timing, my wife decided to fall back on the oldest of women's prerogatives. She changed her mind. The novelty of the whole water birth idea had evaporated. She wanted to give birth on Terra Firma. The bucket relay was suddenly over.

"I want to get out. I NEED to get out," she said with a remarkable decisiveness given the circumstances. And just in case we either hadn't heard or didn't agree, she was already on the move.

You may be amazed to hear that when women are in the throes of childbirth, their mind doesn't always turn to the laws of physics. But laws they were, and there was no bending them. As my wife tried to stand to get herself out of the pool, she leaned on the edge with one hand taking all her weight. This therefore also meant that one spot on the rim of the paddle pool was also bearing the full burden.

A neat v-shape appeared and the water knew exactly what

to do. It had seen its escape route and was making a break for it. I knew this was meant to be a water birth, but no one said anything about flooding the entire house. I had no intention of being swept away and missing the whole thing.

I pushed back on the outside of the pool as Vicki stepped in to offer a shoulder to lean on instead. My wife took the shoulder with one hand and transferred the rest of her weight from the edge of the pool to my head with the other. I was useful at last! Between the two of us, we took sufficient weight to stem the tide and stop the pool from bursting its banks.

The bed was close at hand and my wife gingerly slid a leg over the edge of the pool and made the short lunge. To an outsider it would have looked like a comparatively simple maneuver, but to me this seemed a very dangerous moment for her to be spreading her legs.

Dr. Paul was back in position, another pair of surgical gloves snapped into place. I was sure I could see tangible signs of relief on his face that my wife had decided to get out of the water and make his job a heck of a lot easier. She may have been on all fours on a bed (and I hadn't seen that in a long time!) rather than flat on her back in a hospital, but at least she was on dry land, if you excluded a not-so-small puddle that had managed to make it to freedom.

Events now seemed to have taken on a life of their own. Even Dr. Paul seemed very much an observer rather than a participant. Nature had taken control and my wife's body was doing what it needed to do. She was riding with it as it controlled her actions rather than vice-versa.

"It's coming!" my wife cried out. "I can feel it. The head's there." Her voice was almost unrecognizable. It had dropped another couple of octaves as she spoke between groans and cries, not so much of pain anymore, but just pure emotion. I was having a child with Barry White.

Vicki's hand rested on my shoulder.

"Are you ready?" she asked me. "Paul, the father wants to catch the baby."

Oh Shit. So I did. Where on earth had that fit of bravado come from when I was asked if I wanted to do this? I had been useless all evening and suddenly I had the most important job of my life, watched by an entourage of experts, almost all of whom had successfully caught babies themselves. I also now had a mangled hand. Did I really need this kind of pressure?

Dr. Paul turned and gave me the knowing smile of someone who has had the privilege of catching many a baby in his time. He took one last look at the scene to check everything was OK, then gently moved to one side to give me room to step in.

"If you're going to catch the baby, then you're going to have to be a lot closer than that," he told me gently.

For some reason I seemed to have been under the impression that my wife was going to fire this baby out like a pinball machine, because I was standing about three feet back from where the action was going to happen. Perhaps it was because I'm English, or stupid, or maybe both, and I thought I was once more on the village green playing cricket, tucked in at second slip and waiting for an edge.

Or to put it into American football parlance, I was standing in the pocket, waiting to receive the ball. I needed to be more like a quarterback waiting to take the snap from the line of scrimmage, hands firmly placed as close between the center's legs as was politely possible. Vicki just laughed and pushed me closer. There was no sense of relief to know I was obviously not the first Dad to make this mistake.

More cries of urgency from my wife alerted me to my duty. By contrast, Dr. Paul's voice was all calm and soothing as he described events and guided me forward.

"Ok, here comes the head. Get your hands underneath it."

And indeed there it was. A tiny little head poking out from within. It was facing toward me and looked like a balloon before it has been inflated — all crunched up into a million little cracks and creases. It was almost impossible to make out any features, but I knew that it was a little face peering blindly at me.

The tiny head squeezed its way out. It didn't yet need my support, but I had my hand there anyway. It was so small it didn't even overlap my palm. I could feel that the baby had hair, but was covered in more fluid than a David Beckham gel commercial. It was all slimy to the touch, like an egg yolk, and just as fragile.

The next push would be the shoulder and after that the baby would arrive faster than Harry Houdini getting out of a straight-jacket. My left hand cradled the head while I waited for the torso to slide out.

I was ready, and I wasn't, all at the same time. I didn't

even know what emotion I was feeling. I think somewhere I had them all going at once. Excited, nervous, amazed, scared, happy, worried, tense, elated, stressed, calm. The whole selection was swirling around in my head, with each feeling taking turns to be uppermost in my mind. But there was no time to dwell on it. One thought seemed to overpower all the others: "Whatever you do, don't drop it."

As the baby's shoulder appeared, it broke the vacuum and I was proved right about one thing. I was suddenly plunged into that scene from Alien.

Apparently the reason my wife's belly had become so big and round was because it contained every revolting sticky, fluid substance ever created by a schoolboy with a chemistry set. Now all that stuff was coming out of my wife at a very rapid pace with a seemingly magnetic attraction for its other creator. It was almost as if it knew it belonged to me.

Dr. Paul, in his infinite wisdom, had sidled another couple of steps away from the firing line and was standing directly behind me. So this was why he had insisted I got a lot closer to the action. I had unwittingly been used as a human shield. Vicki, with equal savvy, was also somewhere behind me. However, her tactic was so that when I instinctively tried to recoil from this stream of putrid essence, I wasn't able to. This was not malice of course, but to ensure I remained close enough to catch the baby, rather than return to my safe position at second slip.

There was no time to be squeamish as the baby was coming out faster than a greased monkey. Rather than being pushed forward, gravity was doing the work and the torso slid almost straight down, with the weight of its little legs then flipping over and into my other hand, like a chef sliding a greasy fried egg onto a plate.

I lurched forward, trying to keep my hands underneath it before this baby became the world's youngest bungee-jumper. It was more slippery than a bar of soap in the prison showers and I was terrified of dropping it. With my gene pool this baby already had enough disadvantages without a bang on its barely formed head. Luckily I, or it, held on and it was still cradled in my hands as I lowered them onto the bed. Wow. It was SO small.

The second part of my task in catching the baby was to be the first person to discover its gender and be able to tell my wife. But I needed to check everything out as it simply didn't seem to be big enough to contain everything required. I stared into the tiny little face. Two ears, two eyes a nose and a mouth. All present and correct. Next, I looked down the body and sure enough, I could see two chubby little arms and a pair of fat little legs. Ten tiny fingers and 10 little piggies on its feet. Everything was where it should be. No, wait, there *was* something missing.

"Darling, it's a girl!" I exclaimed to my wife. "A beautiful baby girl."

֍

"She's got hair!" my wife squealed back as she turned to look.

I wasn't aware that this was a big deal, but to my wife it seemed absolutely vital. Maybe bets had been placed in Las Vegas as to how much hair there would be. All I knew was that I was relieved to have been spared the possibility of failing at yet another important task. I had already proven my propensity to be able to blow 50-50 opportunities, and stating the sex was another possible one. It may seem incomprehensible, but apparently many men get it wrong on first inspection.

As my wife turned to be able to sit and face me, our little offspring, our daughter, was still lying in my hands. It felt as if I needed to be more delicate than when you try to cup water and not let it run out through your fingers. She looked like a raspberry ripple ice cream, all covered in bits of blood and various other unmentionable bodily fluids that stuck to her like Velcro.

"She's got so much hair," my wife repeated. Yes, Ok honey, we knew that already.

She was just amazingly small, but so perfectly formed, like something only the Japanese could engineer. Her tiny little fingers and toes already sported long nails. Her little tongue rasped in and out like a lizard, trying to catch the air and swallow it as she got used to breathing for the first time. She had the biggest eyes, searching the environment to discover where she was and who all these enormous people were. Eyes that were barely a minute old yet seemed to stare at me with infinite wisdom, saying: "I know you — you made me."

"Well, actually honey, you were made in a laboratory dish, but I know what you're getting at," I thought to myself.

Small maybe, but she had the vocal chords of an elephant. Wow, did this girl have some lungs. How could a noise that big have come out of something so tiny? Talk about making an entrance. Perhaps it was a realization that went through a baby's mind after they were born and they make an instant self-evaluation assessment:

"Ok. I was warm and comfortable a minute ago and now I'm not. An awful lot of people seem to be prodding and playing with me. I am not a toy. How come I'm naked? I don't seem to be able to stand. I don't seem to be able to do anything. Hang on. Apparently I can make this violent wailing noise. OK then, let's go with that. And as it's the only thing I can do, let's give it everything I've got."

My wife took her from me, as if the pecking order needed to be established. Nice try mere man, but this is woman's work. Your job is done. She drew the baby to her chest, establishing the skin-to-skin contact that is said to be so important in the early bonding of a child.

"Hello baby," my wife whispered into her daughter's ear. "Look at all the hair you've got."

Oh My God. This poor kid was barely out of the womb and she was going to have a complex about her damn hair. Had my wife been expecting to give birth to Yul Brynner?

Purely by instinct, the baby seemed to know what to do and where do go, inching her way purposefully toward my wife's breast. She had her sights set firmly on that nipple, which to her must have seemed about as big as my celebratory Monte Christo Robsuto cigar that I intended to smoke any minute.

There was something about the sight of a mother and her newborn babe that goes beyond definition. I was able to see past the fact I was in the middle of what looked like a bad traffic accident, with blood and who-knows-what everywhere.

All I could see was a picture of perfect serenity: A woman, naked and exhausted, yet with an expression of immense satisfaction, achievement and unbridled joy. A newborn child with seemingly too much detail crammed into such a tiny little body, oblivious to the cacophony of surrounding noise as it nestled into its mother. The umbilical cord, nature's power cable, still united mother and child and glowed with an incandescence that can only be described as "umbilical blue." Not a color definition Dulux Paints were likely to add to their range anytime soon.

The entourage only added to the scene. Everyone had an expression that signified they had just witnessed something incredible. They had been allowed to share in the most immensely personal experience there was. These were women that did this for a living and had attended countless births, yet each recurrence was as good as the first one, a unique experience that moved them to tears as they shared the joy of bringing a life into the world.

My wife looked at me through teary eyes.

"Thank you. Thank you *so* much."

This was why I loved my wife. In the middle of what must have been an emotional experience of Olympic proportions, from the pain of labor to the ecstasy of childbirth, only moments after seeing and holding her daughter for the first time, she had remembered back to almost a year ago when this journey started with a less than enthusiastic husband. She had not forgotten that this child was my gift to her, the greatest gift one person could ever give another. And she had not forgotten to say thank you.

Of course, being slow on the uptake, it was only just dawning on me now as I looked at my wife and my daughter — my family — that I had got it all the wrong way around.

I had no idea what I was getting into and for the most part had just been dragged along for the ride. It was my wife who went through the injections, the surgery, the doubts, the emotional rollercoaster, the nausea, the bloating, the pain. And at the end of it all, it was not just her that was rewarded with this precious little bundle of life. Often the greatest gift is the one that you give rather than receive, and she had managed that as well.

I had merely given acceptance. My wife had given me a daughter, and by doing so had transformed us from a couple into a family. She had made me a father, the most fantastic job any man will ever have. Yet she was thanking me. It was I who needed to say "Thank You" to her. I was now in her debt forever and would happily spend the rest of my life paying it off. Mind you, I think she still could have let me smoke my cigar inside, just this once.

෧෨

So in my naiveté, I thought we were all done, mission

accomplished. It certainly looked like the celebrations were starting. I dashed to the kitchen and came back with a few bottles of champagne. We did have a bigger entourage than Mike Tyson in his hey-day, after all. Vicki, still imparting wisdom despite us having tried so hard to exhaust her supply, was arranging for bacon sandwiches — there's never a bad time for a bacon sandwich — and as soon as that first aroma of frying bacon wafted into the room, we all suddenly realized how hungry we were.

As I passed the glasses around, everyone had beaming smiles and a look of great satisfaction. Yet no one was actually making eye contact. There was only one focus of attention, even if she didn't know it. I followed their gaze and looked again on my new family. My wife was still absorbed telling my daughter how much hair she had. If my daughter could have spoken, there was no question her first word would have been nipple, as that seemed to be the only thought running through her mind.

Dr. Paul declined his glass of champagne.

"Thanks, but not until after I've birthed the placenta," he said.

There I was thinking the final whistle had gone and now we seemed to be heading for overtime. Scenes from the parenting class came swimming back to me from the depths of my memory. For example, how on earth that woman from class would have managed to have a birth like this with her three dogs still on the bed?

Actually, all I could remember was that I was so repulsed

by the descriptions of what was about to happen that I had switched off and paid no attention whatsoever. Perhaps I could go and get the champagne again, and take a lot longer about doing it this time?

The placenta was attached to the other end of the umbilical cord and had acted like the baby's storeroom during the pregnancy, holding reserve supplies of whatever was needed. Its job was now done, and it needed to come out. Newton was evidently lucky that he stumbled across apples, as apparently his laws of gravity didn't work here, and the placenta would technically also have to be "born."

Instantly, it seemed very fortuitous that I had been ordered to smoke my cigar outside and this seemed the perfect opportunity to do so. Some kind of sixth sense, although my wife thinks I have two at most, was telling me this was not a good place to be. This was definitely a "woman thing."

As I tried to sneak out of the room, I was called back like the dog that ate the dinner. There was to be no escape and no cigar — not even close. I pointed out that if anybody thought I was going to catch this thing, they were sadly mistaken.

Once again, how wrong could I have been? There was another task for which my services were required. While my wife was going to go through a slow-motion replay of giving birth, someone had to hold our new baby. Naturally, I would much rather have done this outside and given her the first taste of second-hand smoke. But of course she was still attached to her umbilical, which didn't come with an extension cord, meaning we would be staying close at hand.

Wrapped warmly in her blanket, she was passed to me as I sat next to my wife on the bed. The blankets swamped her, almost making it look as if she was drowning in them, barely keeping her head high enough to breathe. The good news was her scrunched-up balloon-face had now been inflated, revealing all of her little features. So much detail in such a tiny little face. And she looked so peaceful. She was almost asleep, with her eyes flickering open every so often as if to check whether we were all still there. Best of all was her tiny little mouth, which made faint little sucking sounds and motions, in time to some innate rhythm that seemed to repeat "nipple, nipple, nipple."

She was still covered in all her various bodily fluids, so gently I started to clean her up. Her hair — did we mention that she had hair? — was beyond redemption. Maybe that's why so many babies are born bald. It makes the clean-up easier? So I worked on the simpler bits. Chubby little arms and legs that were so squidgy to the touch it was hard to know whether there were actually any bones in the middle. My wife had apparently given birth to a miniature Michelin Man. Still, it was delicate work and thankfully absorbed my attention sufficiently to be able to ignore whatever was going on next to me. That I did not need to know about and, I promise, neither do you, so consider yourself spared.

Having made her look a lot more presentable, I wrapped her back up in her blanket and left her with a little more breathing room than before. With the extra padding, she fit neatly along my forearm with her head resting at the crook of my elbow. To this day on my desk at work, I have that moment immortalized by a picture of my 15-minute-old baby in my arms.

Yes, I immediately became one of those new fathers I used to consider so pathetic that have pictures all over their desk. As Jerry Seinfeld asked, why did people do that? Were they worried they would forget what their family looked like after a day at the office? Or was it to act as a reminder that they actually *had* a family to go home to and shouldn't go out with the boys for the evening?

"You have tickets for the game tonight? Sure, I'd love to go. Hang on. What's this photo on my desk? Damn. It seems I have a wife and kids. Sorry George, I can't make it."

Looking at my daughter, it was hard to imagine any game being worthy of missing her company.

೦೦

It was good that it only required one hand to hold her, as I still had tasks to accomplish. Next on the list was calling the grandparents. I didn't really care what time it was in either Australia or England, they were going to get disturbed. I called my wife's parents first.

"Hello Pam, it's Simon. You have a beautiful granddaughter."

Various unintelligible and unspellable shrieks and cries followed, until she eventually regained the power of speech.

"That's marvelous. How much does she weigh?"

What? What on earth does that matter, for goodness sake? I

thought. Luckily I was too astonished to actually say anything out loud. I soon discovered it was invariably the first question anybody asks you. Why was that? What was this deal with a baby's weight? Did it portend to how tall, fat, or clever a baby was going to be? Was there a rating system?

Could you imagine if we had to keep doing it throughout our life? Kids at their first day at school: "My name's Mary, I'm six and I weigh forty-three pounds."

"Hi Mary, I'm your teacher Mrs. Wilson. I'm almost 220 pounds, but I'm trying to lose some weight, honest."

Worst of all is that we would breed a bunch of compulsive liars, because nobody tells the truth about their weight. The only person who ever finds out someone's real weight was the guy fitting the safety harness when you went bungee-jumping. You didn't want to be under-estimating your poundage to that guy.

Of course had she been born in a hospital, she would have been whisked off straight away to be tagged and weighed. Now more than ever, with my baby in my arms, I could see at least one advantage in my wife's decision to have a homebirth.

It was usually women that came up with this insightful weight question, so I think there must be a badge of honor as to how much a baby weighed at birth. Or to be more blunt about it, how big it was. Now that was a concept men had more affinity with.

If fortunate enough, a woman would give birth to a small baby, which was naturally the easier option. Tell another mother that your baby was a mere six pounds, or around three kilos, and you could see the unspoken response on their face.

"Six pounds? That's barely a baby. That's like giving birth to a tennis ball. My baby was nine pounds. Like an un-ripe water melon, it was. Almost split me in two. You must hardly have noticed you'd had a baby." Even women who had a caesarian were not averse to saying the same.

So, I was very pleased to say that because we had a home-birth and there were no nurses available to immediately take our baby away to get an answer to this all-important question, I had absolutely no idea what the answer was. I also was completely unable to answer the new grandmother's second question. Although I had to concede, "what's her name?" was a much better one.

I was beginning to wonder why I had bothered calling them, as no doubt had my wife's parents in Australia, where it was 3 a.m.

By the time I called my own parents, things were taking shape. The choice of a name somehow became much easier when you had a face to put it to. Technically, I had been given the final say on a name, once we had painstakingly arrived at a mutually fought-over shortlist. I still couldn't answer the weight question, but I was ready for the other one.

"We're going to call her Reilly."

"You can't do that," my father said from London. "We're not Irish."

I made an immediate apology to my new daughter for the family we had brought her into, but reassured her that they

lived way over on the other side of the world and we wouldn't
have to see them very often.

☾☽

Anyway, while this had been transpiring, all the messy stuff
involving my wife and sacks of mucous membrane and whatever else had been dealt with and cleared away, thank God.
The umbilical cord though, was still attached to the baby.

It must be a traumatic time for a little person to discover
that no sooner are they born, people are cutting bits off them
and throwing them away. We all know the jokes about proud
fathers being just a bit too proud about their offspring's
apparent appendage. Or as Robin Williams so eloquently put
it, "Can't you leave it there a while, let him dream a little?"

Well with us having a girl that was not an issue anyway. Nor
would that particular piece of anatomy be coming anywhere
near her for a couple of decades, if I had my way. The first
young lad who had ideals of introducing my little girl to his
"manhood" was going to get introduced to mine in the form
of a 12-gauge shot-gun and the sound of "How fast can you
run, boy?" ringing in his ears.

Every father out there who has a son, and cannot wait
for him to become a man, should please remember there's
another father out there that has a daughter, who cannot wait
to kill the first boy who cannot wait.

Still, it must be a worry to see the one thing that has
provided you with comfort, nourishment, health and security for the past nine months being taken away. No doubt

this was why it was a job that was designated to the father. So that just in case a newborn baby can already form memories, it would be Daddy, not Mommy that was in the bad books right from the start.

Dr. Paul handed me the scissors. I was pleased to see they were rounded at the end, so at least my shaky hands wouldn't be performing any unscheduled abdominal surgery.

"Are you doing the honors?" he asked. Well at least he had used the word honor. That didn't make it sound so bad. I carefully took the little scissors and Dr. Paul showed me the two points between which I needed to make the cut.

The doula-girls closed in to get a good look. As always, one of them had the video running for posterity. Perhaps Dad would make a mess of things again and they could all have a laugh about it later.

So here we were. The end of our almost year-long "Journey to the Center of the Birth." As the adventure of pregnancy had come to an end, so a new adventure of life had begun. I was about to free my daughter from her nest and transform her into her own little person. Ending the physical tie to her mother, but creating an emotional one to both of her parents. To use a title from the rock band Genesis: And Then There Were Three.

I put the scissors around the cord and squeezed gently. Ok, so it was made of sterner stuff than I thought. Or perhaps it was just that my hands still weren't functioning properly from the mauling they had received earlier? I squeezed again and the blade broke the surface as a drop of lusciously thick, rich red blood oozed out. The really good stuff that had been nourishing her for so long.

There was no turning back now. I pushed the scissors forward and cut again at the cord. I looked at my daughter and she gazed back at me. Was she encouraging me? Were her eyes saying "Go on Dad, it's OK, you can do it. It doesn't hurt." I looked at my wife. She was smiling at me. After what she had just been through in the past few hours, there was no way I was going to make a mess of this.

With the determination and strength of will of the father that I now was, I cut the cord.

"I declare this baby open."

FIN

BIOGRAPHY

BORN IN 1962, SIMON Morse grew up in the outskirts of London, the younger of two children. With a minimum of academic qualifications, he went against his father's advice and wishes and decided to skip university, leaving school at 17 years old, impatient to get out into the real world and make some money.

Money meant banks, and so started a 20-year career in finance that began in retail banking and progressed to the investment arm of the industry. After stumbling into the world of currency trading, he was presented with the opportunity of international travel. After seven years working in London's financial center, he moved to Toronto. Five years in Canada saw a further move to Asia, first in Singapore and then Hong Kong.

But the desire to write had been steadily growing, so despite approaching his 40th birthday, he switched careers and tried his hand at journalism, using his banking background to talk his way into a job covering the financial markets.

It was at about the same time that he got married to his Australian wife, who he had met in Singapore. She is a childbirth educator and runs her own company providing labor support for women. Amazingly, she is still with him to this day.